TIMBER PRESS
POCKET GUIDE TO
Conifers

TIMBER PRESS
POCKET GUIDE TO

CONIFERS

RICHARD L. BITNER

TIMBER PRESS
PORTLAND · LONDON

Frontispiece: *Metasequoia glyptostroboides* 'Ogon', a selection of dawn redwood, in a border

Copyright © 2010 by Richard L. Bitner. All rights reserved.

Published in 2010 by Timber Press, Inc.

The Haseltine Building
133 S.W. Second Avenue, Suite 450
Portland, Oregon 97204-3527
www.timberpress.com

2 The Quadrant
135 Salusbury Road
London NW6 6RJ
www.timberpress.co.uk

Designed by Christi Payne
Printed in China

ISBN: 978-1-60469-170-2

Library of Congress Cataloging-in-Publication Data

Bitner, Richard L.
  Timber Press pocket guide to conifers / Richard L. Bitner.
       p. cm. -- (Timber Press pocket guides)
  Includes index.
  ISBN 978-1-60469-170-2
  1. Conifers--Handbooks, manuals, etc. 2. Conifers--Diseases and pests--Handbooks, manuals, etc. 3. Conifers--Selection--Handbooks, manuals, etc. I. Title. II. Title: Pocket guide to conifers. III. Title: Conifers. IV. Series: Timber Press pocket guides.
  SB428.B553 2010
  635.9'35--dc22
                          2009051600

A catalog record for this book is also available from the British Library.

Dedication

To my friend, Elliot L. Heffner

Acknowledgments

Thank you again to all the people and gardens mentioned in *Conifers for Gardens*, the encyclopedia on which this pocket guide is based. I would also like to thank Oregon designers Bryan and Cassandra Barrett; the affable folks at Iseli Nursery in Portland, Oregon; and Dean Linderman of Leesburg, Virginia, for allowing me access to their wonderful gardens. Thanks to Linda Willms for her skillful editing of the entire Pocket Guide series.

About This Book

The entries in this pocket guide are arranged in alphabetical order by scientific name. Where more than one species is described, a brief introduction to the genus summarizes features common to all the species. As is customary in botanical writing, genus and species names are italicized, cultivar names are not. Furthermore, cultivar names are enclosed by single quotation marks, but selling names and translated names are not.

The botanical nomenclature of some conifers is very confused, and it is not uncommon for the same plant to appear under several different names, or for the originating species of a particular cultivar to be unknown. As DNA studies are carried out in the future, we can expect conifer relationships, and names, to continue to change.

The plant heights and widths given in this book represent what is possible for conifers grown under ideal conditions and are usually expressed as a range. The actual measurements of any plant are dependent on the growing conditions at the site.

USDA hardiness zones are provided as a rough guide to the climate in which a conifer is known to survive. It is often possible to grow conifers in a colder zone, provided they are somewhat protected from the elements. Microclimates also exist in many gardens, and gardeners are encouraged to find such sites and experiment with them.

Occasionally, because of cultural conditions, the photograph of a particular plant will not match the description of that plant. Additionally, some of the photographs do not represent the conifer at maturity or during the season of greatest interest (for instance, those with brighter foliage during a limited time of year). These situations, however, are the exception. Most of the photographs show mature plants at their best season.

One last word. This book was not written to be a field guide for identifying plants. Nonetheless, important ID features are often mentioned to help distinguish similar-looking plants.

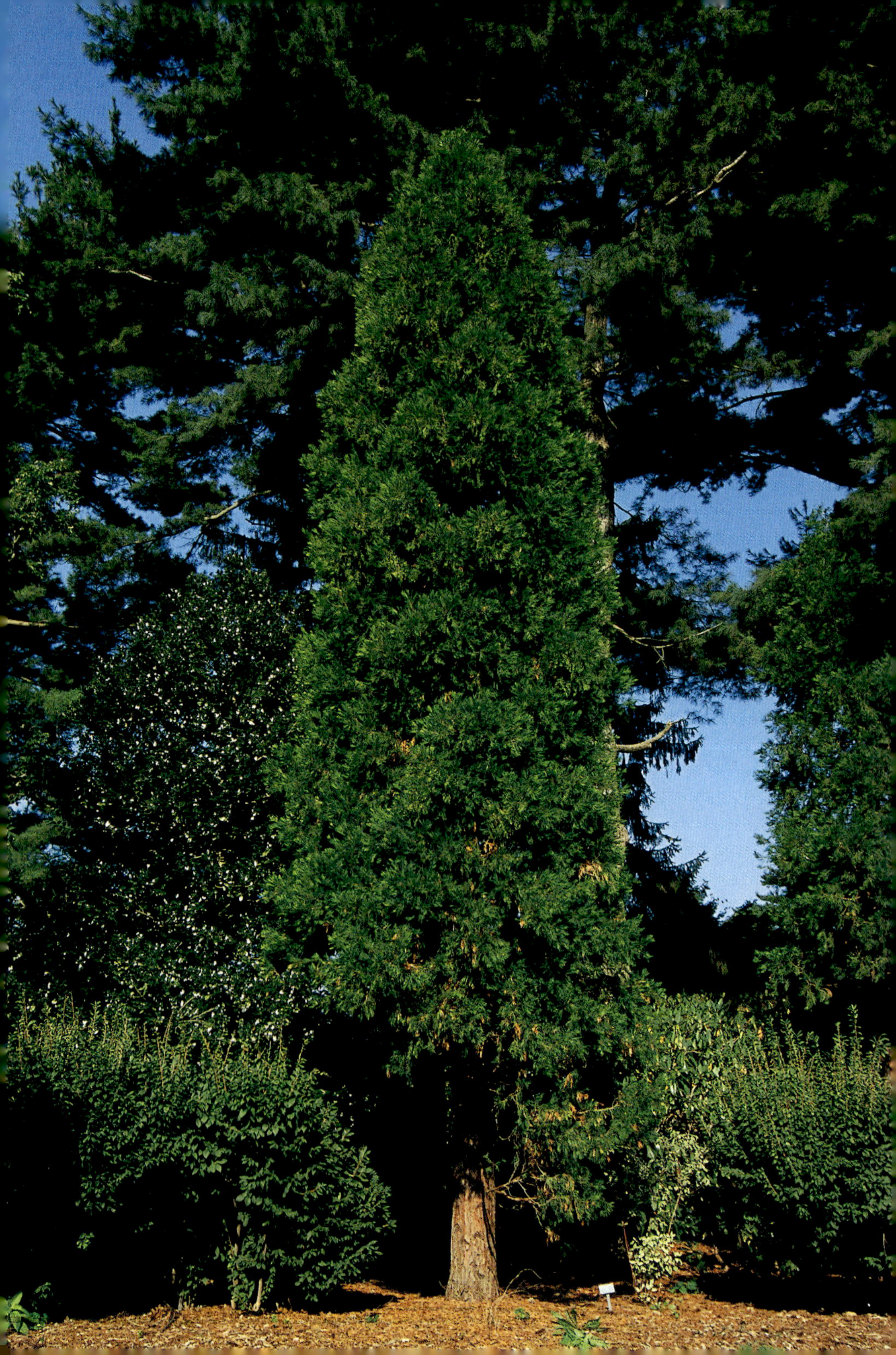

CONTENTS

Preface   9

Introduction   11

Garden Conifers for Specific Purposes and Locations   23

Garden Conifers A–Z   27

Nursery Sources   214

Glossary   216

Further Reading   217

Index   218

Calocedrus decurrens (incense-cedar) is a drought-tolerant Pacific Northwest native that deserves to be more widely planted in the eastern United States. It has a distinctive, narrow habit that makes it useful for smaller properties and it adapts to a wide range of cultural conditions.

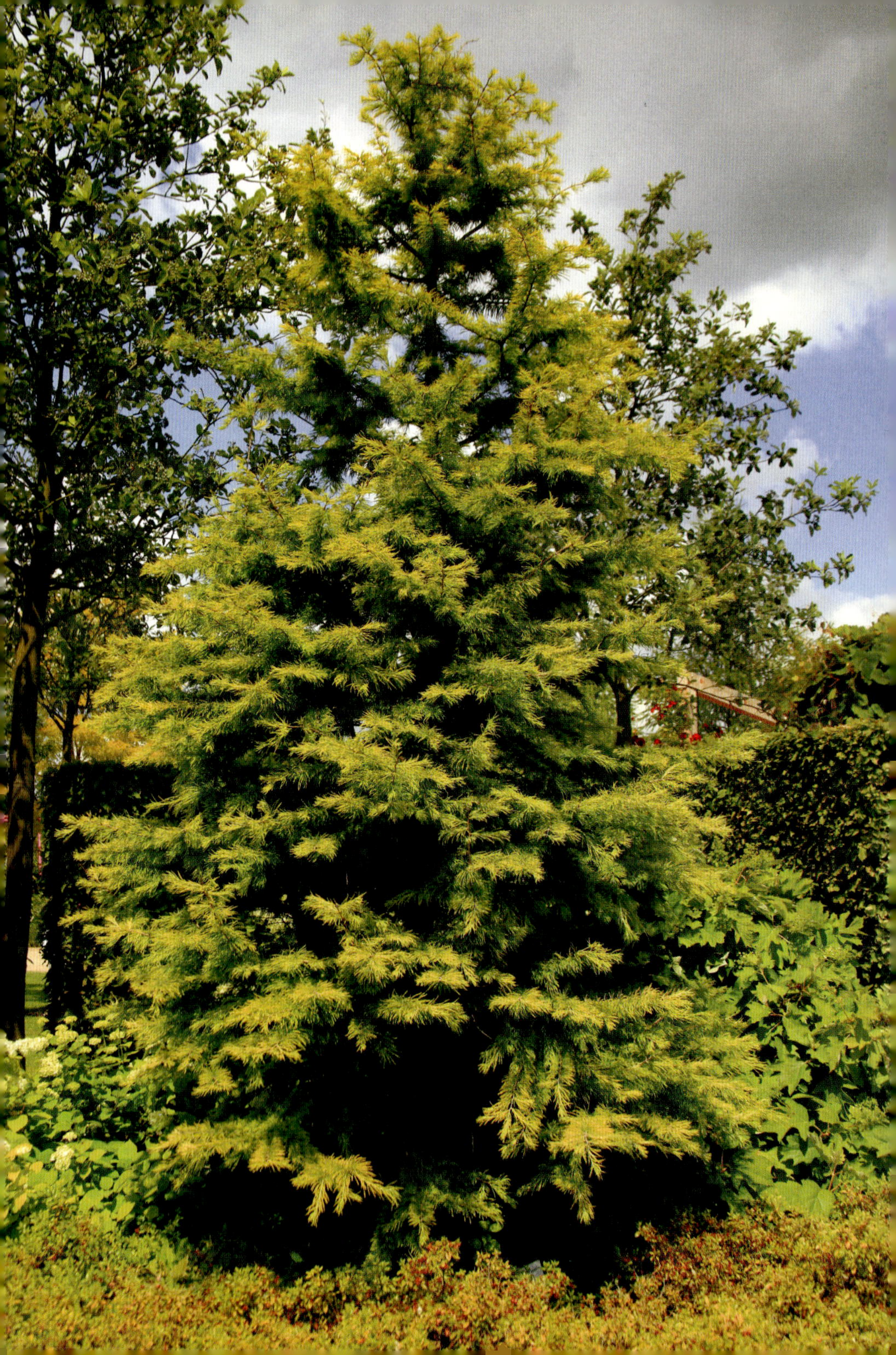

PREFACE

My love affair with conifers began in the 1990s, when I took a course on the subject at Longwood Gardens, Kennett Square, Pennsylvania. Like many gardeners, I thought of conifers primarily as plain-green blobs used to hide the foundations of homes and other buildings, and occasionally as a solitary pyramidal accent in the middle of a large expanse of grass. The same plants seemed to be used again and again and again, reflecting the limited selection of conifers available at many nurseries. Furthermore, many of the conifers that I had seen were poorly placed in the landscape and now, having outgrown their allotted space, were subjected to severe pruning of their unwanted limbs until they could no longer be considered "ornamental."

The Longwood course changed my thinking about conifers and introduced me to the great diversity of shapes, textures, and colors in this large plant group. I began taking photographs of unusual junipers, spruces, pines, yews, arborvitaes, and hemlocks as well as common varieties when they were used well in the landscape. I quickly accumulated a library of many thousands of photographs. My enthusiasm must have been evident to others, for I was asked to teach the very course at Longwood that sparked my interest in conifers. Currently, I split my time equally between teaching anesthesiology and writing, photographing, or teaching about conifers.

My interest in conifers focuses on integrating them in the landscape with other woody plants and with perennials rather than isolating them. My hope is that this pocket guide to conifers will help the reader—whether beginning or avid gardener, landscape designer, nursery tradesperson, or horticulture student—make better choices.

The foliage of *Pseudolarix amabilis* (golden-larch) is beautiful and eye-catching whether it is emerging mint-colored in the spring or displaying brief golden fall color.

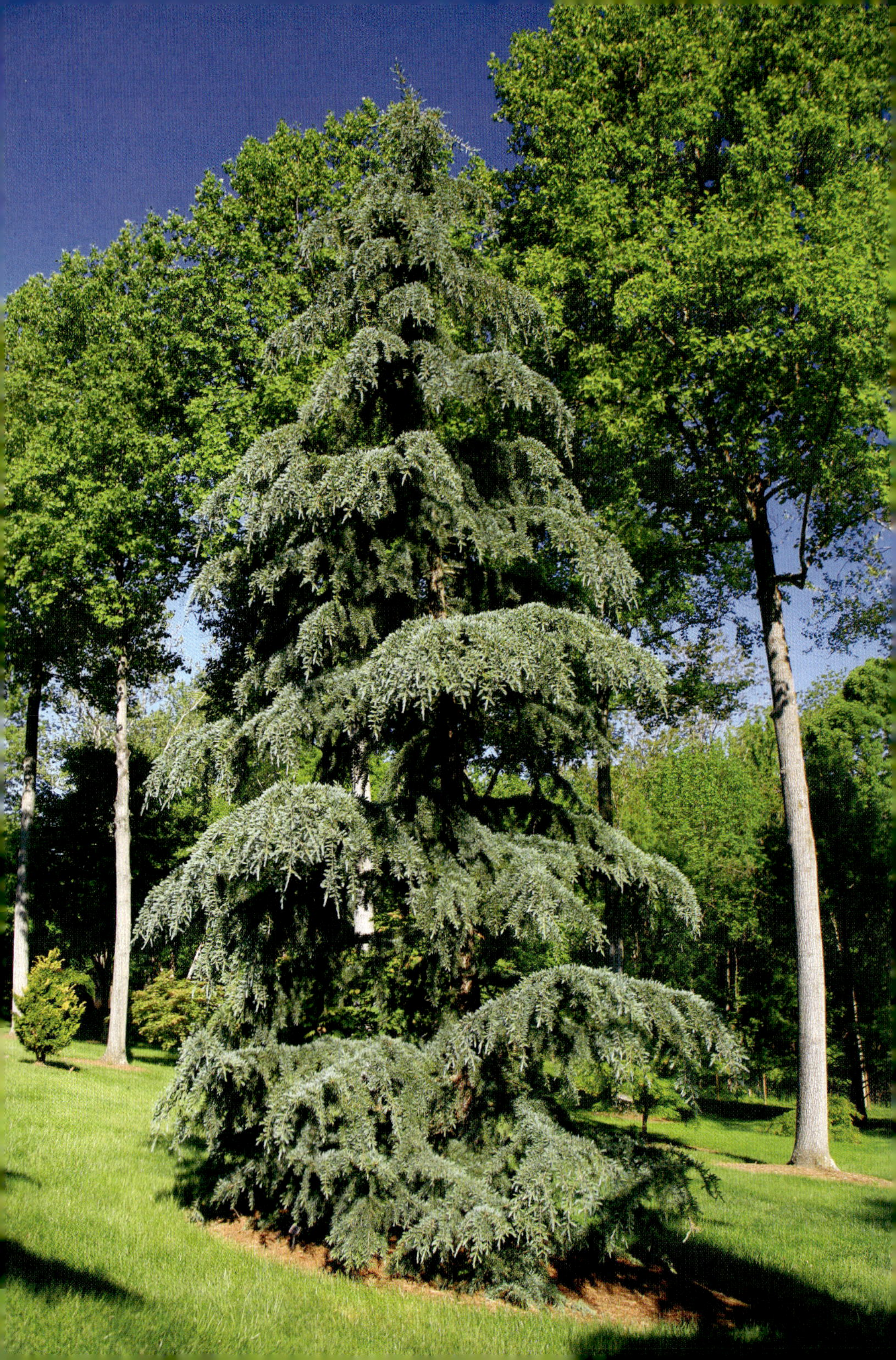

INTRODUCTION

Conifers are often the number-one choice for gardeners and home-owners who are looking for problem-free, drought-resistant, low-maintenance plants for their landscape. Conifers seldom need to be pruned, watered, or fertilized, and they never need to be divided. These plants are unquestionably utilitarian, but they are also thoroughly ornamental, providing year-round color and interesting texture wherever they are planted. Furthermore, they happen to be permanent, which makes selecting the right plant even more critical.

This book is intended to remove the element of uncertainty from selecting a conifer that may alter a landscape for years to come. It focuses on the best cold-hardy conifers for homes and gardens. All of the major conifer groups—firs, spruces, pines, junipers, yews, redwoods, arborvitaes, hemlocks, and more—are represented.

But first, what is a conifer? What sets it apart from other trees and plants?

Conifer Botany

A brief glance at conifers suggests that they cannot simply be described as evergreen trees with needles. In fact, their group name refers to the characteristic that sets all of these plants apart. The word "conifer" comes from the Latin word meaning "to bear cones." A conifer bears cones, and those cones hold its seeds. If you shake a typical cone as it matures and opens, seeds will fall out.

Plants that produce seeds encompass most of the plants on earth and are placed into two divisions: angiosperms and gymnosperms. The angiosperms, which comprise the largest group of plants, have so-called covered seeds. Think of an apple or a pumpkin, where the seeds are embedded in the fruit. The gymnosperms, which include conifers, have so-called naked seeds. There are fewer than a thousand species of gymnosperms, representing only half a percent of known plant species.

The mature, fertilized cone is the conifer's female "fruit" (although technically conifers do not "flower" and therefore cannot bear "fruit"). In most species, cones are woody structures. Not all conifers produce cones that look like the classic pinecone, however. Sometimes the seed is simply enclosed in a fleshy coat. Separate male "flowers" grow in the shape of a tiny cone or a catkin and provide the pollen to fertilize the female cone. In this book these staminate cones (male) and pistillate cones (female) are referred to (and often illustrated, because they are ornamental) as the pollen-bearing cones and seed-bearing cones, respectively.

Pollination in conifers is always dependent on wind currents to blow the abundant yellow pollen from the pollen-bearing cones to the seed-bearing cones. Fertilization takes place, and the seeds mature. This process can take a season or several years. The seeds are then released to drop or are dispersed by wind or by birds. Some seeds are held tightly in closed cones until prompted to open by a forest fire.

Most species of conifers are monoecious; that is, they produce both pollen-bearing cones and seed-bearing cones on the same tree. Other conifers, such as junipers and yews, produce these cones on different trees; these plants are dioecious. Some cones, such as those of the pines, carry numerous seeds, while the juniper "berry" cone, for instance, usually encloses only a single seed.

Not all conifers have needlelike leaves that are held singly or in bundles (examples are spruces and pines); many have tiny flat scalelike leaves

---

The long soft foliage, graceful overall appearance, and more pendulous whiplike leader distinguishes deodar cedar from the other cedars. Shown here is *Cedrus deodara* 'Karl Fuchs'.

that tightly surround the twig (as in arborvitaes). When conifer seeds germinate, they have juvenile or needlelike foliage. Sometimes this needlelike foliage is maintained throughout the life of the plant, but generally the adult or scalelike foliage develops. These leaves are exceedingly small, densely crowded, and overlapping (junipers are the best illustration of this). There are cultivars that retain their juvenile foliage, forms that have both juvenile and adult foliage, and those that have all adult foliage.

The flat needles of *Abies nordmanniana* (Nordmann fir)

The scalelike foliage and fleshy cones of *Thuja orientalis* (oriental arborvitae)

Conifers in Nature

Various species of conifers, especially those in the pine family (Pinaceae), are the dominant forest cover over much of the Northern Hemisphere. There are extensive forests of junipers and cedars in northwestern North America. Many conifers have exceptionally wide natural ranges; *Juniperus communis* (common juniper), for instance, is circumpolar. Others, such as the numerous conifers that occur only at specific elevations of California, have relatively restricted natural ranges; these conifers are not adaptable as garden plants and are not discussed in this book. An exception is *Picea pungens* (Colorado spruce), which is found only in mid- to high-elevation zones in five western states, yet is widely planted and adapted across Europe and North America.

The Naming of Conifers

Latin is the universal language of plants. In addition to a Latin, or scientific name, many plants have a common name. Common names can be useful but are often confusing, especially with conifers. A good example in the English language is the common term "cedar" which has been used for at least six different genera (*Calocedrus*, *Chamaecyparis*, *Cryptomeria*, *Juniperus*, *Taiwania*, and *Thuja*) besides the true cedars of the genus *Cedrus*.

The Latin name, consisting of two parts, places the conifer within a larger system of nomenclature. This binominal system was invented by Swedish botanist Carolus Linnaeus (1707–1778) who cataloged in Latin all the plant and animal species known in his time. Translation of the Latin name often reveals characteristics of the plant.

The first part of a Latin plant name refers to the genus: *Juniperus*, *Cedrus*, *Pinus*, and so forth. A genus is a group of plants with very similar characteristics. The second part of the Latin plant name is the specific epithet, commonly called the species. A species is a group of genetically very similar plants that are distinct from other species in the genus. Some genera (the plural of genus) have dozens of different species; other genera comprise only one species. The genus name is capitalized and the species name is not; both words are written in italics, as in *Pinus strobus*.

Latin plant names often include a third part. This third name could refer to a subspecies or variety—plants found under special circumstances in nature—in which case it, too, would be written in italic. An example is *Cedrus libani* subsp. *stenocoma*, a hardier form of the cedar of Lebanon.

The most common third part to a Latin plant name is the designation of a cultivar, or cultivated variety. These plants are in some way different from the usual species—perhaps displaying blue foliage rather than green, or having a slower growth habit—and are usually propagated by grafting or by rooted cuttings to maintain this characteristic's ornamental interest. The cultivar name is written in Roman type and is enclosed in single quotes, as in *Pinus strobus* 'Elf'. The cultivar name often reveals a characteristic of the plant selection.

Prior to 1959, cultivar names were designated in Latin: *Pinus strobus* 'Contorta'. Today the name must be in the language of the person who introduced or named the plant, as in *Abies koreana* 'Silberlocke', which was introduced by Horstmann Nursery of Germany.

When two species interbreed in the wild, a hybrid is produced. The offspring's name is written with an × between the genus and species to signify this: *Juniperus* ×*pfitzeriana*, for example, is a cross between *J. chinensis* and *J. sabina*. There is no strictly right or wrong way to pronounce these Latin names, but every syllable must be spoken.

The earliest properly published name is the one that has to be used. Occasionally a cultivar, or even a species, that has been published and

Garden conifers are available in a varied palette of forms, colors, and textures that complement deciduous shrubs and herbaceous plants.

sold under a familiar name for decades requires a name change because research has shown that it was recorded earlier with a different name. The experts who catalog plant names and characteristics and dictate these matters are called taxonomists. The Royal Horticultural Society (RHS) took responsibility as the international registration authority for conifers in 1964 and has since been accumulating and publishing information. The International Conifer Register (ICR), published by the RHS, is an attempt to provide precise, stable, and internationally acceptable nomenclature for this plant group. Other standards for conifer names include *The World Checklist of Conifers* by Humphrey Welch and Gordon Haddow from 1993, and the *RHS Plant Finder*, which is published annually.

Some cultivar names will not be listed or considered legitimate with these authorities but will nevertheless be in widespread use. If I have observed plants so labeled in arboreta and collections and listed in several conifer specialty nursery catalogs, I have included them in this pocket guide under the commonly accepted name.

Conifers are grown all over the world. Those who pursue unusual selections are naturally eager to introduce and sell them. Confusion, duplication, and discrepancies are bound to occur from time to time. My apologies for entry names that some factions might consider erroneous. The situation is likely to get even worse. DNA studies of plants are becoming very important tools in resolving these issues and can lead to a total reordering of sections of botanical classifications.

Growing Conifers

Perhaps more than any other group of plants, conifers are selected without much thought and are inappropriately placed in the home landscape. They are often considered merely useful, low-maintenance shrubs to situate next to a building to hide its foundation. Or a single specimen of *Picea pungens* (Colorado spruce) is placed in the middle of the front yard and overshadows the house years later. Despite this misuse, garden conifers are available in a varied palette of forms, colors, and textures. With some care in selection, these evergreens can provide interest and color year-round, especially if dwarf and slow-growing cultivars are combined with deciduous shrubs and herbaceous plants.

Conifers are not particularly finicky. Some with variegated foliage appreciate a little shade; others need protection from drought or harsh winds. Most *Abies* (fir) and *Picea* (spruce) species certainly do better in cooler climates and will sulk in areas with hot, humid summers, but in general conifers are adaptable to a wide range of growing conditions.

Conifers are generally not considered shade plants and will do best when given full sun exposure. Nonetheless, there are a few species suitable for the gardener wishing to place conifers in a shady spot.

Like most plants, conifers do best in moist, well-drained, neutral to slightly acid soil, but they are usually able to survive whatever circumstances the gardener provides. Newly planted specimens need to be watered, but once established, conifers tend to be rather drought-tolerant, an important consideration in this era of global climate change. Depending on their branch structure, some conifers will suffer damage from heavy, wet snow. Most dislike poor drainage, but *Taxodium distichum* (bald-cypress) will tolerate standing water part of the growing season.

Cold hardiness zones are listed for each species described in this book, but hot, humid summers might affect a plant's survival more than low winter temperatures. Unlike deciduous trees, evergreen conifers do not have to grow a whole new set of leaves every spring; therefore their demands for nourishment are correspondingly less. They seldom need fertilizer. They lead rather frugal lives.

The range of plants described in this volume shows that there are possibilities for sun and shade, wet and dry situations, and even for alkaline soils. There is likely to be a suitable conifer for any design specification.

Growth rates and ultimate size are listed for most of the plants. Precise dimensions and growth rates are not given, however, because

Metasequoia glyptostroboides (dawn redwood) is a magnificent tree when given adequate space. It is readily available, fast growing, and adaptable wherever planted.

many cultivars will be planted in markedly different conditions from the area in which they were studied and introduced. Sometimes a plant has been observed for only a few years before being made available for sale, and the ultimate size is not yet known. Descriptions based on nursery-grown plants are subject to error. Sometimes a gardener buys a mislabeled container. Occasionally slower-growing cultivars will revert; that is, out of the desired, compact, congested foliage will appear a faster-growing branch. These branches must be pruned off, or they will dominate the plant.

Conifers are best moved or planted when relatively small. It is wise to plant them in late spring or in early fall. Select plants that display the proper shape and healthy foliage. Remember that most conifers will not regrow lost branches, especially at the base.

The same principles should be followed with conifers as with any plant a gardener wants to grow. First, assess the various aspects of the climate, site, and soil. Then choose a plant that suits the site and intended purpose. Finally, grow the plant well, attending to its needs.

Using Conifers in the Garden

Conifers come in all shapes and sizes from tall and narrow to rounded, weeping, or even low-growing. The classic shape of conifers is pyramidal, making them ideal as focal points in large formal gardens. Many are fine hedging plants, providing shelter, windbreaks, and sound barriers. Some would say they are overused as groundcovers. Conifers can be grown in containers and are widely grown as bonsai. They are a requisite in Asian-style gardens and indispensable for creating topiaries.

There are limitless choices of slow-growing conifers of all shapes for suburban landscaping, urban vest-pocket gardens, and grave plantings. Some conifers grow only several feet in a hundred years, others 4 ft. (1.2 m) in one growing season. Careful consideration must be given to the ultimate height and spread when placing these plants; unlike perennials, the gardener does not have the luxury of moving conifers here and there with each new growing year.

Conifers are not forgiving of crowded conditions. They want space to make their statement. Branches die when subjected to shade; however, most genera have slow-growing cultivars that keep their scale over many years in a mixed border, where they provide structure throughout changing seasonal displays.

A golden-leaved conifer paired with a purple coneflower

Chamaecyparis obtusa (Hinoki falsecypress) is a favorite conifer of bonsai enthusiasts.

In addition to their shapes and sizes, conifers are desirable plants because of their varied foliage colors and textures. Colors range from different hues of green, gray, or blue to exotic golds and silvers. There are even variegated forms. A few have foliage that changes color seasonally. Deciduous conifers add to the parade of fall colors.

Textures vary, from needles that can act as effective barriers to soft flat fronds that invite touching. Several conifers could be grown for their beautiful bark, notably *Pinus bungeana* (lacebark pine). In climates that support them, conifers associate beautifully with heaths and heathers. The very slow-growing selections are indispensable in trough and rock gardens.

Conifers are more than ornamentals. Not to be overlooked is their considerable value for wildlife. These plants not only provide protection and shelter for birds, but many of them also supply cones with edible seeds for birds and mammals. Many conifers are capable of producing both wood and nonwood products that have been of great benefit to society, and they provide flavorings and medicinal products. There have been traditional uses of every part of the tree—foliage, bark, roots, resin, seeds, and cones. Pine bark mulch is now widely used to satisfy the mulching frenzy of suburbanites.

Conifers have been revered and utilized by many cultures, notably the First Nations peoples of the Pacific Northwest. Many conifers have a rich mythology and folklore. They appeared on colonial flags and are depicted in the visual arts (the cypress paintings of Vincent van Gogh) and music (*The Pines of Rome* by Ottorino Respighi).

Witches' Brooms

The countless available conifer cultivars, mostly dwarf or slow-growing, originate from several sources. Some of these cultivars are collected in

Container-grown conifers

the wild and propagated by seed or by rooting cuttings from the plant. Similarly, many are discovered among the rows of thousands of seed-grown container plants in nursery production. Occasionally distinct changes in color or growth rate occur on normal branches of an established tree. These sports can be propagated and nursery stock obtained.

Perhaps the most celebrated way to find new types of conifers is by searching for witches' brooms. These are congested bundles of usually small-needled growths that are attached to normal branches, particularly those of *Pinus* (pine) and *Picea* (spruce) species. There are various explanations of why they occur, including bud mutations, parasites, viruses, fungi, insects, or other pathology. When witches' brooms are collected and propagated, they usually remain dwarf. Sometimes they produce cones and viable seed which, in turn, can result in other dwarf selections. Since the number of years (or decades) these plants are grown and evaluated before being made available for the home gardener will vary greatly, it is easy to understand that there will all too often be similarity of forms, confusion of names, and duplication.

Pests and Diseases of Conifers

Good cultural practice is the most effective way to avoid problems with pests and diseases in conifers. When grown under appropriate conditions, conifers can deal with periods of excessive heat, cold, drought, storm damage, and minor infestations of pests and diseases. Stressed plants cannot.

Stress is caused by poor soil, poor drainage, air pollution, salt, damage to roots, damage to bark (usually from mowers or string trimmers), soil compaction, improper pruning, storm damage, and pesticides. With conifers, excessive moisture rather than moisture deficiency is a common circumstance that leads to disease problems.

For best results, select conifers that are suitable to your site and practice proper planting methods. It is especially important that these trees not be planted any deeper than they were growing originally. It is essential to provide a regular supply of water during the first year while the plant is getting established. Most conifers grow best in slightly acid soil having a pH of 5 to 6. Disease problems are more likely when pH levels are higher. Unnecessary supplemental fertilization should be avoided.

Ironically, vigorous, fast-growing trees are more susceptible to fungus infestations, the most common of coniferous diseases. Most diseases are caused when fungi and other organisms enter

Witches' brooms usually occur high up in trees, but here one is growing in front of a pine.

the unprotected wood and the process begins. Wounds caused by mowers repeatedly hitting a tree trunk take a long time to heal.

Inspect conifers regularly to detect pest and disease problems early, when straightforward procedures can avoid an escalation of the situation. Often disease-resistant varieties are available.

Animal Damage

Deer and other hoofed browsers can be the most troublesome pests in gardens and arboreta, particularly in eastern North America. Browsing occurs throughout the year, but especially during the cold season, when deciduous plants are bare. Deer are chiefly attracted to *Taxus* (yew) and *Thuja* (arborvitae) species, but one can never consider a "deer-resistant" plant list trustworthy. Fencing at least 8 ft. (2.5 m) high is the only reliable way to exclude these expert jumpers. Prized plants can be caged to keep deer out. Many deer repellents are marketed; success with these products is apparently related to a willingness to reapply them regularly and after heavy rain.

Small rodents like mice, voles, squirrels, and rabbits damage conifers by chewing on trunks and roots under the snow and eating bark, twigs, and buds. Again, fencing and chemical repellents are useful. Many public gardens maintain cats in the garden to control these pests. Watchful dogs, perhaps especially beagles, are very good for keeping all intruders out of the garden, provided they are given proper housing and are in the garden at night.

Insect Pests

Most insects found in the garden are not pests at all, but are beneficial. Even those that are considered harmful will not be damaging unless they

Conifers in a trough garden

Conifers in a display garden mulched with gravel

are present in large numbers. It is best not to reach for a pesticide immediately upon spotting a potentially damaging insect since this can lead to other problems. Most pesticides are harmful to beneficial insects as well as to livestock, fish, and humans. Often physical methods of control or changing cultural practices will take care of the situation. Vigilant monitoring for the extent of a pest population before resorting to chemicals is sensible.

When chemicals are necessary to control damaging insects, they should be the appropriate ones for the pest identified, applied at the correct time in the pest's life cycle, and in a proper dose. Pesticides are poisons. In the United States they are regulated by the federal government and by individual states. Before using a pesticide, check with local authorities, county agents, a university cooperative extension service, or an agricultural experiment station to determine current use regulations. Do not apply pesticides on windy days or when honeybees are pollinating plants. Wear protective equipment when spraying, and wash exposed skin thoroughly when finished. Toxic chemicals should be stored in their original containers, out of reach of children, pets, and livestock, and away from food and feed. Dispose of empty containers in a safe manner.

Seasonal Needle Drop

Home gardeners often become concerned when they observe needles on their "evergreen" turning brown and dropping off. The needles of conifers have varying life spans and will drop after one to several years. *Pinus strobus* (eastern white pine), for instance, drops its two- to three-year-old needles in the autumn, and this will be quite obvious on a mature plant. The shedding of needles is less noticeable in other popular genera like *Picea* (spruce). One need only confirm that the needle loss is from old growth. Needle loss from the tips of branches would be a reason for concern.

Pathogens

The most common disease-causing organisms in conifers are fungi. Other diseases are caused by bacteria or viruses. Fungi will often cause a conifer to shed needles. Yellow spots will appear on the needles, which eventually turn brown and are shed. Sometimes tiny black fruiting bodies of the fungus are noticed.

Numerous blights can occur, including diplodia tip blight (*Sphaeropsis sapinea*; syn. *Diplodia pinea*) and brown spot (*Mycosphaerella dearnessii*; syn. *Schirrhia acicola*). The twig tips and needles are afflicted and eventually large areas of foliage turn brown, especially on the lower branches, and are shed.

Dozens of fungi can infect injured tree bark, causing a blistered area, or canker. These diseased areas are very noticeable and often have resin oozing from them. Fusiform rust (*Cronartium*), juniper blight (*Phomopsis*), and cytospora canker (*Leucocytoma kunzei*) are some of the most troublesome pathogens of conifers. Canker diseases will weaken and kill branches as the fungal pathogen invades the sapwood.

Normal loss of pine needles

Canker diseases are difficult to manage. A fungicide spray program by a certified administrator might be necessary to control repeated cycles of infection. The best way to prevent these diseases is to grow conifers under proper cultural conditions, providing good air circulation, and avoiding bark wounds, drought, and environmental stresses.

Average Annual Minimum Temperatures for Plant Hardiness Zones

Temperature (°F)	Zone	Temperature (°C)
Below −50	1	Below −46
−50 to −40	2	−46 to −40
−40 to −30	3	−40 to −34
−30 to −20	4	−34 to −29
−20 to −10	5	−29 to −23
−10 to 0	6	−23 to −18
0 to 10	7	−18 to −12
10 to 20	8	−12 to −7
20 to 30	9	−7 to −1
30 to 40	10	−1 to 4
Above 40	11	Above 4

To see the U.S. Department of Agriculture Hardiness Zone Map, go to the U.S. National Arboretum site at http://www.usna.usda.gov/Hardzone/ushzmap.html

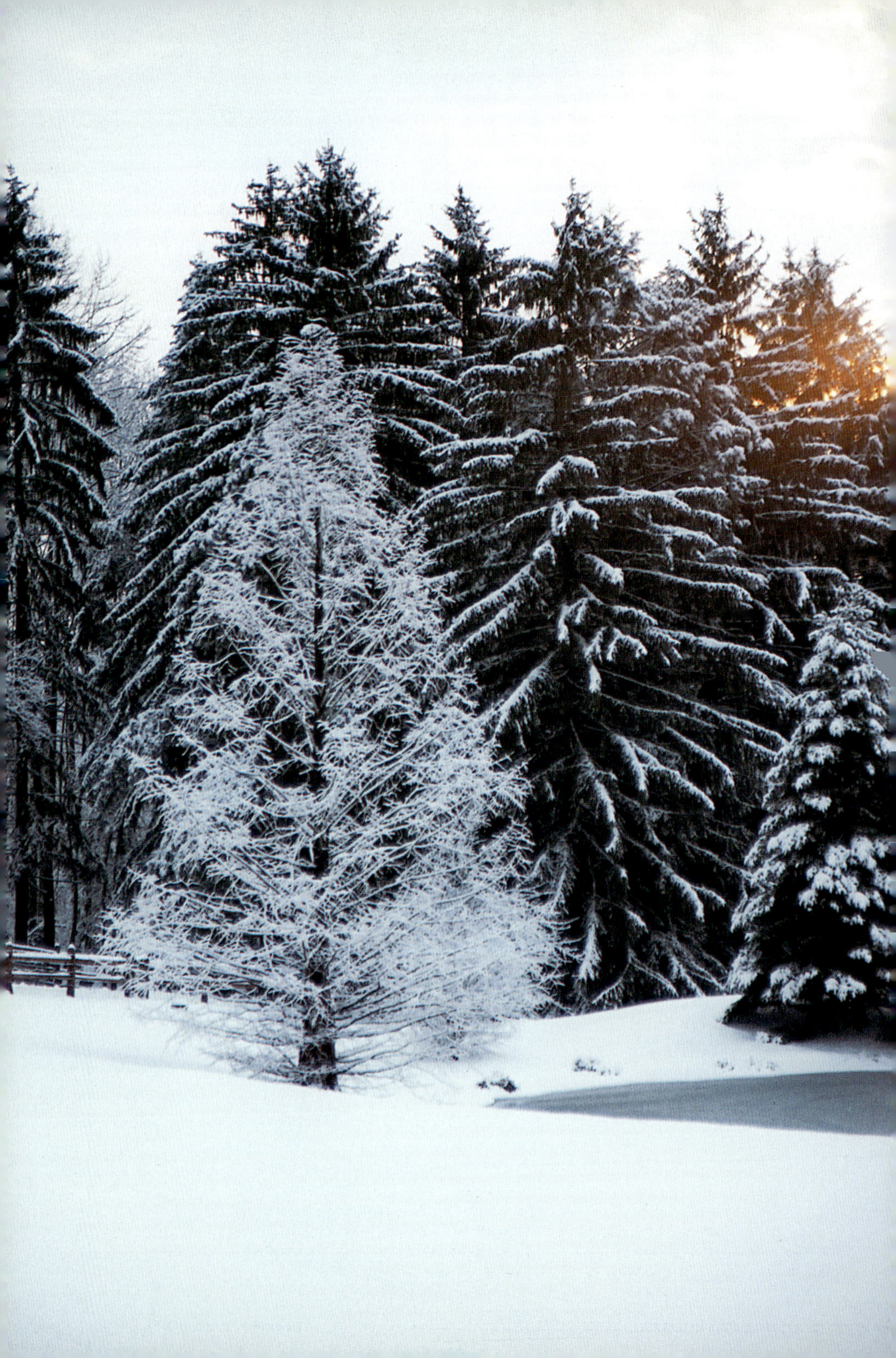

GARDEN CONIFERS FOR SPECIFIC PURPOSES AND LOCATIONS

Gray to Silver-Gray or Blue-Gray Foliage

Cultivars labeled 'Glauca', 'Glabra', or 'Argenteo-', or with "blue" or "silver" in their name.

Abies concolor
Abies lasiocarpa var. arizonica
Chamaecyparis lawsoniana 'Oregon Blue'
Chamaecyparis pisifera 'Boulevard'
Juniperus squamata 'Blue Star'
Juniperus virginiana 'Grey Owl'
Picea pungens

Yellow or Gold Foliage

Cultivars labeled 'Aurea' or 'Lutea', or with "gold" in their name.

Chamaecyparis obtusa 'Crippsii'
Cryptomeria japonica 'Sekkan-sugi'
Taxus baccata 'Standishii'
Thuja plicata 'Zebrina'

Upright, Narrow Habit

Cultivars labeled 'Columnaris' or 'Fastigiata'.

Calocedrus decurrens
Cephalotaxus harringtonia 'Fastigiata'
Ginkgo biloba 'Princeton Sentry'
Picea omorika
Pinus cembra
Pinus nigra 'Arnold Sentinel'
Taxodium ascendens 'Nutans'
Taxus baccata 'Standishii'
Taxus ×media 'Hicksii'
Thuja occidentalis 'Smaragd'

Weeping Habit

Cultivars labeled 'Pendula', or with "weeping" in their name.

Abies concolor 'Blue Cloak'
Chamaecyparis nootkatensis
Picea abies 'Gold Drift'
Pinus banksiana 'Uncle Fogy'
Thuja orientalis 'Franky Boy'

Ornamental Bark

Pinus bungeana
Pinus densiflora
Pinus sylvestris
Sequoiadendron giganteum

Rapid Growers

Cryptomeria japonica
Larix decidua
Larix kaempferi
Metasequoia glyptostroboides
Picea abies
Pinus strobus
Pseudotsuga menziesii
Taxus baccata
Thuja occidentalis
Thuja plicata
Tsuga canadensis

Tolerant of Somewhat Moist Soils

Abies
Chamaecyparis pisifera
Juniperus communis
Larix laricina
Metasequoia glyptostroboides
Picea abies
Picea glauca
Taxodium
Thuja occidentalis

Snowfall highlights the distinctive branching structure of *Metasequoia glyptostroboides* (dawn redwood) in the foreground, while slightly weighing down the usually upturned branches of *Picea abies* (Norway spruce) behind it.

Tolerant of Moist to Wet Soils
Larix laricina
Metasequoia glyptostroboides
Taxodium

Tolerant of Sandy, Dry to Poor Soil
Abies concolor
Cupressus arizonica
Juniperus
Picea omorika
Picea pungens
Pinus banksiana 'Uncle Fogy'
Pinus mugo
Pinus nigra
Pinus sylvestris

Tolerant of Compacted Soils, Drought, and Heat
Ginkgo biloba

Tolerant of Alkaline Soil
Cedrus atlantica
Cephalotaxus harringtonia
Chamaecyparis lawsoniana
Chamaecyparis nootkatensis
×Cupressocyparis leylandii
Ginkgo biloba
Juniperus
Picea omorika
Pinus leucodermis
Pinus mugo
Pinus nigra
Taxus baccata
Thuja
Thujopsis dolabrata

Tolerant of Clay Soil
Abies
Chamaecyparis
Juniperus
Larix
Picea pungens
Pinus nigra
Taxodium
Taxus
Thuja

Tolerant of Acid Soil
Cupressus arizonica
Juniperus
Picea pungens
Pinus aristata 'Sherwood Compact'
Pinus cembra
Pinus leucodermis
Pinus mugo
Pinus parviflora

Tolerant of Seacoast Conditions
Araucaria araucana
Cedrus deodara
Cryptomeria japonica
×Cupressocyparis leylandii
Cupressus macrocarpa
Juniperus chinensis
Juniperus conferta
Juniperus horizontalis
Juniperus virginiana
Picea glauca
Picea pungens
Pinus cembra
Pinus leucodermis
Pinus mugo
Pinus nigra
Pinus parviflora
Pinus sylvestris
Pinus thunbergii

Tolerant of Light Shade
Cephalotaxus harringtonia
Chamaecyparis obtusa
Cryptomeria japonica
×Cupressocyparis leylandii
Microbiota decussata
Picea abies
Picea orientalis
Sciadopitys verticillata
Taxus
Thuja
Thujopsis dolabrata
Tsuga canadensis

GARDEN CONIFERS FOR SPECIFIC PURPOSES AND LOCATIONS

Tolerant of Urban Pollution

Araucaria araucana
Cedrus atlantica
Cephalotaxus harringtonia
Chamaecyparis
Cryptomeria japonica
Ginkgo biloba
Juniperus
Larix kaempferi
Metasequoia glyptostroboides
Picea abies
Picea omorika
Picea orientalis
Picea pungens
Pinus cembra
Pinus densiflora
Pinus mugo
Pinus nigra
Pseudotsuga menziesii
Sciadopitys verticillata
Sequoiadendron giganteum
Taxodium distichum
Taxus baccata
Taxus cuspidata
Thuja
Thujopsis dolabrata
Tsuga canadensis

Tolerant of Cold to Zone 3

Juniperus communis
Juniperus scopulorum
Microbiota decussata
Picea glauca
Picea pungens
Pinus aristata 'Sherwood Compact'
Pinus cembra
Pinus flexilis
Pinus mugo
Pinus strobus

Tolerant of Cold to Zone 4

Abies concolor
Abies nordmanniana
Ginkgo biloba
Juniperus chinensis
Juniperus horizontalis
Juniperus virginiana
Larix decidua
Larix kaempferi
Picea abies
Picea pungens
Thuja
Tsuga canadensis

Tolerant of Heat to Zone 9

Araucaria araucana
Cedrus libani
Cephalotaxus harringtonia
Cunninghamia lanceolata
Cupressus arizonica
Juniperus
Taxodium distichum

Suitable for Hedges

Calocedrus decurrens
Chamaecyparis lawsoniana
×*Cupressocyparis leylandii*
Cupressus macrocarpa
Juniperus
Larix decidua
Picea abies
Pinus nigra
Taxus
Thuja
Thujopsis dolabrata
Tsuga canadensis

Favorite Holiday Trees

Abies concolor (concolor fir)
Abies koreana (Korean fir)
Abies nordmanniana (Nordmann fir)
×*Cupressocyparis leylandii* (Leyland cypress)
Cupressus arizonica (Arizona cypress)
Juniperus virginiana (eastern red-cedar)
Picea abies (Norway spruce)
Picea glauca (white spruce)
Picea pungens (Colorado spruce)
Pinus strobus (eastern white pine)
Pinus sylvestris (Scots pine)
Pseudotsuga menziesii (Douglas-fir)

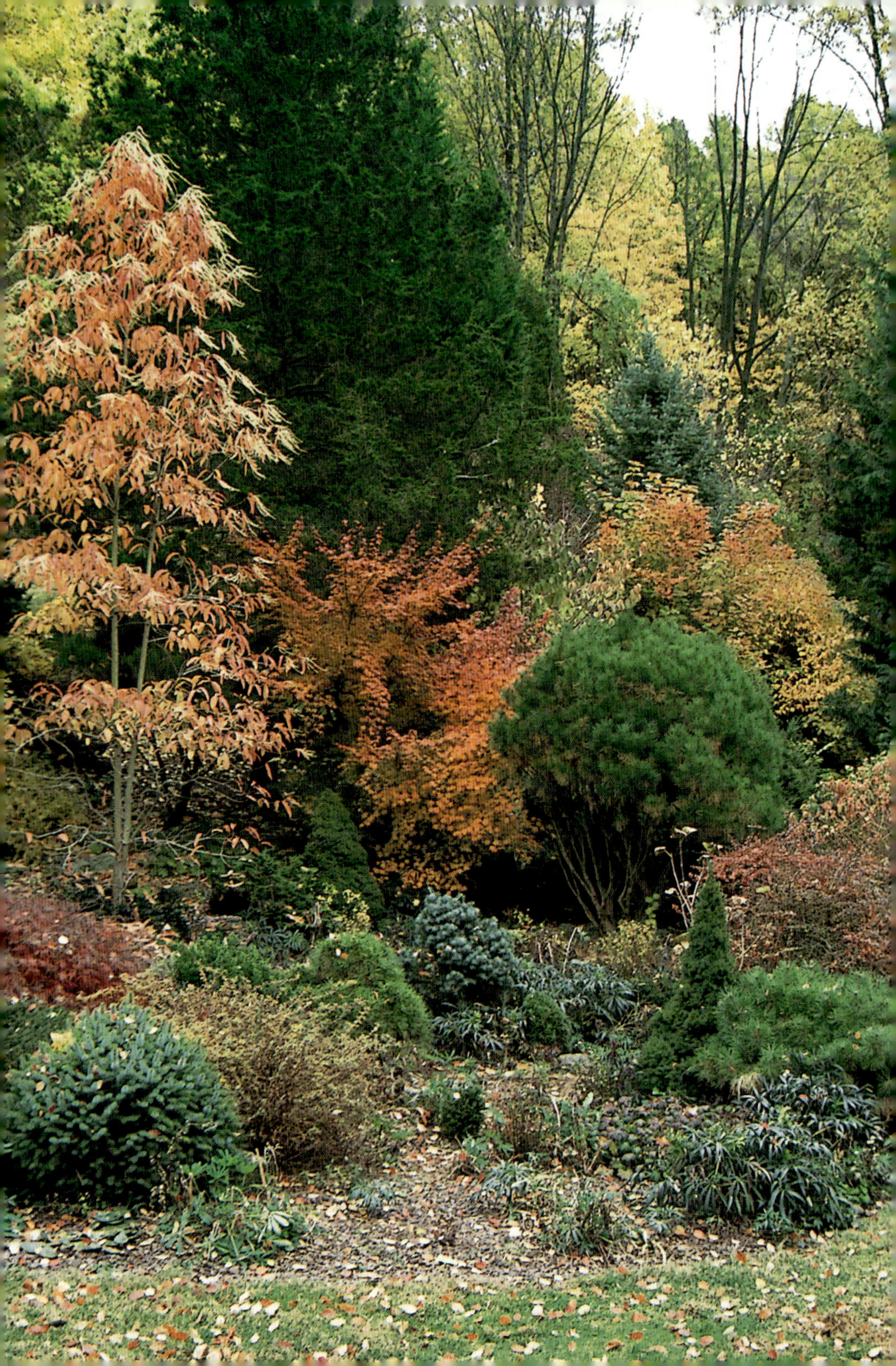

GARDEN CONIFERS A–Z

ABIES
Fir

The approximately 50 species of firs originate in eastern Asia and North America, with a few species in Europe and northern Africa. They prefer cool mountains with sufficient moisture and good drainage. Nine species are native to the United States.

Firs have splendid form: spearlike tips above regular layers of whorled branches and straight trunks from base to tip. They make impressive trees and can be used in groupings in public landscapes, near large buildings, or as screens. Firs shed huge weights of snow quickly and easily. Although most species are of forest size and too large for the home garden, numerous dwarf selections are prostrate, compact, or pendulous.

Description

The trunks of firs are smooth, gray, and dotted with blisters which sometimes ooze aromatic resin. The leaves are evergreen, needlelike, and generally flat in cross section. The needles are arranged spirally and are usually blunt-tipped. Many are green and grooved on one side and have numerous rows of white stomata below. The stems are smooth. The needles usually have a citrusy odor when bruised.

Firs are monoecious. Their seed-bearing cones are barrel-shaped and stand upright on the branches, usually high in the upper crown of the tree. As these cones mature over one year, they glisten with exuded drops of resin. Eventually they disintegrate on the tree. The pollen-bearing cones occur on the same tree and are found on the underside of the lower crown branches.

ID Features

One way to distinguish *Abies* from *Picea* (spruce) is by the cones: *Abies* cones are held upright, *Picea* cones hang down. Another way to distinguish the two genera is to pull a needle off its twig. If no piece of the twig epidermis comes off with the needle, the plant is a fir. A third ID feature is the stem: *Abies* stems are smooth; those of *Picea* are warty.

Abies bark

Conifers provide year-round interest when integrated into the border.

Abies needles and smooth stem

Cultivation

Firs have shallow roots and do not tolerate urban pollution. They require full sun, and some prefer cool summers. Firs are difficult to establish in areas that experience high humidity and hot summer nights, such as the southern United States. They flourish in gravelly soil or other sites with excellent drainage.

Abies seed-bearing cone

Abies seed-bearing cone disintegrating on the tree

Pests and Diseases

Firs generally have few pests and diseases.

Uses

The wildlife importance of firs is only moderate. The evergreen foliage of young trees is useful to mammals and game birds for cover, especially in winter. Firs are used for nesting by many bird species, notably robins and mourning doves, whose first nest of the season is normally built before hardwood trees produce leaves.

Fir seed is readily eaten by chickadees, purple finches, and crossbills. The seeds are also sought by squirrels and chipmunks. Grouses make fir needles a major part of their diet. Hoofed browsers, particularly northern deer and moose, resort to fir foliage as a large part of their winter menu.

Firs are not commercially important in the timber industry. Many are grown as holiday trees. They are ideal because of their natural shape, fragrant needles in shades of green or blue-green, good needle retention, and nice branching arrangement for holding ornaments.

Abies concolor
Concolor fir
Zones 4 to 7

The concolor fir is native from Oregon to Colorado, Utah, Arizona, New Mexico, and California. This dense, pyramidal tree with a rather rigid, stiff appearance reaches 50 ft. (15 m) tall by 20 ft. (6 m) wide, growing 8 to 12 in. (20 to 30 cm) a year. The needles are 2 to 3 in. (5 to 7.5 cm) long. They are soft, flat, and waxy, bluish on both sides, and curve upward. They are sharp at the tip and two-ranked along the stem and have a citrus fragrance when crushed. The stem is smooth with disc-shaped leaf scars after the needles drop. The olive-colored cones are cylindrical, 3 to 4 in. (7.5 to 10 cm) long, and held erect on the branch. They disintegrate when mature and are rarely seen. The bark is gray and on aged specimens becomes thick and horny with deep furrows and ridges.

This fir is one of the most adaptable of the firs. It is somewhat tolerant of drought and salt. It also withstands heat and air pollution better

Abies concolor

than most firs. It should do well on any well-drained soil in full sun. It should not be planted in heavy clay.

The concolor fir is an excellent choice for the designed landscape where a blue pyramidal tree is desired. It remains far more attractive over its longer life span than a Colorado spruce (*Picea pungens*) and is softer to the touch. The wood is soft and very light, useful only for making boxes and for pulp.

'**Blue Cloak**': a weeping form selected for its blue foliage, grows to 30 ft. (9 m) tall by 15 ft. (4.5 m) wide in 30 years and retains its lower branches.

'**Candicans**': one of the bluest forms, fast-growing, upright, and conical, reaching 40 ft. (12 m) tall.

'**Compacta**': irregularly rounded and slow-growing, reaches 2 ft. (0.6 m) after many years, nice for the rock or small garden, once known as 'Glauca Compacta'.

'**Conica**': a compact, conical dwarf with steel-blue 1 in. (2.5 cm) needles, leader grows 6 in. (15 cm) a year.

'**Wattezii**': prostrate and spreading with pale gray-blue needles. When propagated by grafting, it is sometimes labeled as 'Wattezii Prostrata'.

Abies concolor 'Candicans'

Abies concolor 'Conica'

'Winter Gold': green needles turn gold in winter, grows 6 in. (15 cm) a year.

Abies koreana
Korean fir
Zones 5 to 8

This garden-worthy fir is native to the mountains of southern Korea. It grows slowly to 15 to 35 ft. (4.5 to 10.5 m) in a pyramidal form with horizontal branches. The needles are ½ to ¾ in. (1.2 to 2 cm) long with a rounded or notched apex, dark green above with two distinct white bands on the underside. This elegant species is admired for the silvery underside of the foliage of many cultivars and its 1½ to 3 in. (3.5 to 7.5 cm) long, cylindrical, round-ended cones, which range in color from dark purple to blue and often appear even on trees under 3 ft. (0.9 m) tall, a very appealing quality. The bark is dark tan-brown and slightly resinous.

Grow the Korean fir in full sun in a cool, moist location. It tolerates wind but does not like wet feet or compacted soil. It is more heat-tolerant

Abies concolor 'Wattezii'

Abies koreana seed-bearing cones

than most firs and is an excellent accent choice for the home landscape.

'**Cis**': miniature and bushy with rich dark green needles, grows 1 in. (2.5 cm) a year.

'**Goldener Traum**': dwarf and low-spreading with golden foliage in winter, sold in the United States as "golden dream."

'**Prostrate Beauty**': spreads irregularly, grows slowly, has no central leader, produces colorful cones early.

'**Silberkugel**': dwarf and rounded displaying bright green needles with silver undersides, good for trough and rock gardens.

'**Silberlocke**': tightly curved-in foliage exposes silvery undersides, much slower growing than the species, tree becomes more dense with age and displays beautiful purple cones in spring. Choice.

'**Starker's Dwarf**': dense and ground-hugging, eventually becoming conical, produces cones early, has dark glossy green foliage.

Abies lasiocarpa
Alpine fir
Zones 5 and 6(7)

Found from Alaska south to British Columbia and Alberta and south through the Rocky Mountains of Idaho, Montana, Wyoming, Colorado, Utah, and Nevada into Arizona and New Mexico, the alpine fir is the most widespread fir in western North America. It is slow growing and has a distinct habit: very slender, erect, and rigid, like a pencil. All but the lowermost branches are extremely short. This is the tree so beloved by photographers to frame their views of snow-capped mountains. In mountain meadows, it reaches 50 to 75 ft. (15 to 23 m) tall; at high elevations, however, it can be hardly taller than a person (note the term "alpine" in a strict botanical or ecological sense applies to the tundra zone above the timberline).

The stiff needles are 1 to 1¾ in. (2.5 to 4.5 cm) long, deep blue-green with a notched tip. The new growth has a silvery sheen with fine white bands on all sides. The foliage grows out from all sides of the twig and looks brushed up-

Abies koreana 'Prostrate Beauty'

Abies koreana 'Silberlocke'

ward on the twig. The cones are violet-purple, densely clustered, and 2¼ to 4 in. (5.5 to 10 cm) long. The bark is smooth, thin, and pale gray with resin blisters, sometimes with a reddish inner bark showing through fissures.

This fir does not survive forest fires. The wood is light, soft, and knotty and useful only for pulp.

Variety *arizonica* (corkbark fir): found in the mountains of southern Colorado, into New Mexico and Arizona, grows to 75 ft. (23 m) with a thick trunk and corky creamy white branches, silvery gray needles are 1 to 1½ in. (2.5 to 3.5 cm) long, cones are small.

Variety *arizonica* **'Compacta' (compact Rocky Mountain fir):** slow-growing and densely pyramidal, foliage soft gray-blue, bark whitish, also listed as *Abies lasiocarpa* 'Arizonica Compacta'.

'Martha's Vineyard': a medium-sized selection with a neat habit and pale blue new growth, reaches 30 ft. (9 m) tall.

'Mulligan's Dwarf': upright and conical with dense, dark green needles.

Abies nordmanniana
Nordmann fir
Zones (4)5 to (6)7

This stately and elegant fir is native to the Caucasus Mountains of southeastern Europe and western Asia. It has a dense pyramidal form with branches that tend to droop and fully

Abies lasiocarpa var. *arizonica* 'Compacta'

Abies nordmanniana

Abies nordmanniana 'Golden Spreader'

clothe the tree to the base. It reaches 50 ft. (15 m) tall by 20 ft. (6 m) wide, growing 8 to 12 in. (20 to 30 cm) a year. The needles are ¾ to 1¼ in. (2 to 3 cm) long. They are shiny dark green above with two white bands below (see photo on page 12). The flat needles are notched at the tip and often point toward the tip of the twig. There is an orange-peel fragrance when they are crushed. The stem is smooth, with disc-shaped leaf scars. The cones are cylindrical, up to 6 in. (15 cm) long, and held erect on the branches. They are rarely seen since they disintegrate while on the tree. The bark is charcoal-gray.

Grow the Nordmann fir in well-drained, acid soil in full sun. It tolerates heat better than most firs and is an outstanding choice for a specimen or windbreak in the larger designed landscape. It is one of the few fir species that tolerates hot, humid summers.

'Barabits': dwarf and broad-spreading, also called 'Barabits' Compact' and 'Barabits' Spreader'.

'Golden Spreader': a slow-growing, flat, round, spreading form with bright golden yellow foliage in winter, grows 3 in. (7.5 cm) a year, leaders should be cut out. Choice.

Abies pinsapo
Spanish fir
Zones 6 to 8

The Spanish fir is a relatively slow-growing species that is native to both sides of the Strait of Gibraltar. It can reach 70 ft. (21 m) tall in the wild but is unlikely to exceed 45 ft. (14 m) under cultivation. Since it is native to a region of hot summers, it is a fir better suited for growing in more southern areas.

These conical trees are usually branched to the ground and have beautiful short blue-green

Abies pinsapo foliage and cones

needles that spread radially from the branches at nearly right angles and are ¼ to ¾ in. (0.6 to 2 cm) long, stiff (sharp and prickly to the touch), and plasticlike with white bands on the underside. The upright seed-bearing cones are 5 to 7 in. (12.5 to 18 cm) long, light brown in color, and appear in spring.

The best performance is in full sun on well-drained soils. This fir is useful in formal garden designs because of its distinctive habit. Crushed in water, the twigs yield a kind of soap.

'Aurea': a weak-growing shrub to 25 ft. (8 m) tall with waxy needles that are blushed golden yellow in full sun.

'Glauca': a form with distinctive short, rigid, frosty blue, waxy needles that whorl around the stems, reaches 15 ft. (4.5 m) tall in 15 years and eventually 60 ft. (18 m). Makes a distinctive focal point in the garden.

'Horstmann': an attractive low-spreading compact dwarf with stiff blue foliage, grows 4 in. (10 cm) a year and is useful for trough gardens.

Abies pinsapo 'Glauca'

Araucaria araucana
Monkey puzzle tree, Chile-pine
Zones 7 to 9

The unusual monkey puzzle tree is native to the hilly slopes of the former Arauco Province of Chile, where it can grow to 100 ft. (30 m) in height. In cultivation it seldom exceeds 30 ft. (9

Araucaria araucana

m). It always has a single very straight stem with the branches whorled around it. It is slow-growing and very open and symmetrical in youth.

With age the top becomes dome-shaped above bare trunks. It has sharp, spiny-tipped dark green leaves that are arranged spirally around the stem. The leaves are leathery and overlapping and persist for many years. Mature specimens tend to lose their lower branches. The trunk is said to resemble an elephant's foot. It suckers from its roots. The horizontal branches become downward-sweeping branches that curve up at the tip like the tail of a monkey. The cones are very large, 5 to 8 in. (12.5 to 20 cm) long, and mature over three years. They break apart while on the tree. The pollen- and seed-bearing cones are usually on separate trees. The large seeds (up to 300 per cone) were an important food source to indigenous peoples, who roasted them.

The monkey puzzle tree prefers moist soil and protection from harsh winds. It does not tolerate pollution. It is often grown as a garden specimen in the Pacific Northwest and California and is frequently planted in England. The tree is usually grown as a specimen or in a grove.

Calocedrus decurrens
Incense-cedar
Zones 5 to 8

Incense-cedar (not a true cedar) is native to the Cascade Mountains in Oregon southward into California and Nevada. This species (formerly *Libocedrus decurrens*) can live more than 500 years and grows to 150 ft. (46 m) tall under favorable conditions in its native habitat. In cultivation it rarely exceeds 50 ft. (15 m).

It is a slender tree with a spirelike top. The trunk is straight and tapers from a broad base. The trunks are often fluted and buttressed. The branches emerge perpendicular to the trunk and then ascend abruptly upward. In time the crowns become open and irregular.

The lush and lacy deep glossy green foliage has closely overlapping, scalelike leaves that look like they were pressed with an iron. The leaves are arranged in a whorl of four around the branchlet, giving it a jointed appearance. Some of these leaves can be ½ in. (1.2 cm) long. The foliage is held erect and is similar on both sides, with no apparent top or bottom. The leaves give off a pungent spicy aroma when crushed.

The bark is cinnamon-red, fibrous, furrowed, and reportedly 3 to 8 in. (7.5 to 20 cm) thick; this enables mature trees to survive wildfires.

The pollen-bearing cones appear on the ends of lateral branches and shed their pollen in early winter. The ¾ to 1 in. (2 to 2.5 cm) seed-bearing cones appear at the tips of the previous season's growth and have six pointed scales with two large scales that bend back from the axis of the cone, looking like a duck's bill. The seeds germinate readily, even in shade.

Calocedrus decurrens bark

Calocedrus decurrens 'Berrima Gold'

Calocedrus decurrens 'Maupin Glow'

Incense-cedar grows in a wide range of soils. It is very drought-tolerant, inhabiting areas that receive as little as 15 in. (38 cm) of annual rainfall. Nevertheless, young plants should be watered during dry spells. Incense-cedar grows well in sun or light shade, in a wide range of conditions. It makes a very handsome tree in the designed landscape and deserves to be more widely planted (see photo on page 6). A single specimen lends a formal effect. A grove of these is dazzling.

'Aureovariegata': a slow-growing, columnar, variegated form with leaves splashed with yellow and green.

'Berrima Gold': a slow-growing, bright gold form that looks deep gold to orange in the winter. It is popular in England.

'Maupin Glow': a yellow-tipped form.

CEDRUS
Cedar

The genus *Cedrus* includes only four species, three of which are in cultivation. The four are native to eastern Mediterranean, northern Africa, and the Himalayas. Although cedars are widely planted, they are mainly suitable for large gardens or public landscapes. Frail-looking young specimens develop into wide-spreading stately trees with massive trunks as they age.

Description
The needles are arranged in spirals on the growing shoots and appear in rosettes on spur shoots on older stems. Cedars vary in the length and the color of their needles, depending on the provenance of the tree.

Cultivation
Cedars adapt to a wide range of soils, but are not reliably cold hardy below zone 5.

ID Features
Cedars are difficult to identify by their cones, which are all the same shape. And, because both *Cedrus atlantica* and *C. libani* can achieve enormous size, distinguishing between them is made even more difficult.

A magnificent cedar easily dwarfs a colorful maple

Uses

Cedar wood has been prized since antiquity; it is sweet-scented, oily, durable, uniform, and easily worked. It has poor steam-bending qualities but dries easily with a tendency to warp. The heartwood is light brown in color. It is durable but resistant to preservative treatment. It is used for construction, bridges, garden furniture, fences, gates, and paneling in railroad sleeping cars.

Cedrus atlantica
Atlas cedar
Zones 6 to 9

Cedrus atlantica is considered by some authorities to be a variety or subspecies of *C. libani*, to which species it is closely related. Native to the Atlas Mountains of Morocco and Algeria in northern Africa, the Atlas cedar is pyramidal when young but becomes wide-spreading with age, to 60 ft. (18 m) tall by 40 ft. (12 m) wide. It grows a bit faster during youth than in maturity. It is open and skeletal-looking early on, but after several decades is handsome beyond description.

The Atlas cedar typically grows one trunk, with branches extending off the main trunk at a 45° angle. The branches become horizontal as they extend, but the tips are pendulous. The tree grows 6 to 12 in. (15 to 30 cm) a year. The prickly needles are $3/4$ to 1 in. (2 to 2.5 cm) long and are borne spirally on young shoots and then whorled, 30 to 45 needles on spur shoots, further back on the stem. The foliage is green to blue-green year-round. The erect pollen-bearing cones are relatively large at 1 in. (2.5 cm) long and appear in late summer. The much smaller immature seed-bearing cones are hidden among the needles on spur shoots. The mature cones are egg-shaped, 3 in. (7.5 cm) long, and borne upright. Like those of all *Cedrus* species, they disintegrate when ripe the third year. The bark is charcoal-gray and becomes rugged with age. Rows of sapsucker holes are often seen.

Cedrus atlantica should be grown in full sun on well-drained soils. It does not accept shade. It tolerates drought and some salt. It is especially tolerant of chalky soil since in its native habitat it grows on dry limestone. It occasionally suffers some winter injury in colder zones and should be protected from winter winds. It is considered difficult to transplant. Trees that have been regularly

Cedrus foliage and erect cones

Cedrus pollen-bearing cones appear in the fall

root-pruned prior to moving will do best. The pollen is not considered particularly allergenic.

Cedrus atlantica is not very attractive in youth but in 20 years becomes an imposing and picturesque silvery specimen in the larger landscape. It is also frequently seen as an espalier and in bonsai. In cultivation, forms with blue foliage are preferred, but stands of wild trees have green foliage. Dwarf, weeping, and fastigiate cultivars are available.

'Aurea': a conical form with short golden yellow needles in the first year's growth, reaching 25 ft. (8 m) tall.

'Aurea Robusta': upright and broadly conical with golden-tipped branches, more vigorous than 'Aurea', reaching 30 to 60 ft. (9 to 18 m) tall.

Cedrus atlantica 'Aurea Robusta'

'Cheltenham': powder blue needles, upright habit with a central leader, the contorted branches lean downward, grows 10 ft. (3 m) tall by 5 ft. (1.5 m) wide in ten years.

'Fastigiata': a large, dense form with sharply ascending branches that form an upright column, the needles are blue-green, reaches 40 ft. (12 m) tall by 30 ft. (9 m) wide.

Cedrus atlantica 'Cheltenham'

Cedrus atlantica 'Fastigiata'

Cedrus atlantica 'Glauca Pendula'

'Glauca Pendula' (weeping blue atlas cedar): serpentine leader with weeping branches and steel-blue needles, needs to be supported and well positioned, once established it grows 8 to 16 in. (20 to 40 cm) a year. This cedar is stunning trained to form an archway or embrace a pergola or fence. A living sculpture.

Cedrus deodara
Deodar cedar, Himalayan cedar
Zones 7 and 8(9)

Cedrus deodar, the least hardy of the true cedars, is native to high elevations in the Himalayas of Afghanistan, Pakistan, Kashmir, and western Nepal. Although variable, the habit is generally pyramidal with a drooping leader, a horizontal branching pattern, and gracefully pendulous branch tips. The mature plants are flat-topped. They reach 50 to 70 ft. (15 to 21 m) tall in cultivation but have been recorded as tall as 150 ft. (46 m).

The needles are 1¼ to 2 in. (3 to 5 cm) long (longer than *Cedrus atlantica* or *C. libani*) and have a bluish cast. They are arranged alternately and singly on current growth, and spirally on short spurs with 15 to 30 needles per whorl on older growth. The needles are diamond-shaped (not square) in cross section. The long soft foliage, graceful overall appearance, and more pendulous, whiplike leader are good ID features for distinguishing it from the other cedars. Pollen-bearing cones appear in autumn at the end of short shoots and are 2½ in. (6 cm) long. The more limited seed-bearing cones ripen in the autumn following pollination and break apart the next year. They are barrel-shaped, 3 to 5 in. (7.5 to 12 cm) long. The bark is smooth and gray on young trees but with maturity has wide black to pink-gray furrows with short scaly ridges.

The deodar cedar should be planted in full sun in well-drained, average soil. It tolerates heat well but should be protected from winter winds in colder areas. The tree grows vigorously when young and has a narrow crown and branch tips that hang down noticeably. After 20 years, the tree can become rather ragged-looking, especially if denied sufficient moisture. Give it space.

The deodar cedar should be grown as a large specimen for its magnificent, graceful habit with hanging branches. Its timber was traditionally used for shipbuilding in India.

'**Aurea**': fast-growing, golden yellow needles in spring turn yellow-green the rest of the year, best color in full sun. See photo on p. 49.

'**Devinely Blue**': wide-spreading, flat-topped mound with pale gray-green new growth, drooping branch tips, usually listed this way although it is named for a person named Divine.

'**Feelin' Blue**': dwarf spreading form with gray-blue foliage, reaches 1 ft. (0.3 m) tall by 3 ft. (0.9 m) wide in ten years.

'**Glacier Blue**': slowly spreading mound, icy blue foliage.

'**Gold Cone**': narrow upright form with pendulous branch tips, outer needles golden yellow, inner blue-green, fast grower, reaches 8 ft. (2.3 m) tall by 4 ft. (1.2 m) wide in ten years.

'**Golden Horizon**': semi-prostrate and flat-topped with gracefully weeping branches,

Cedrus deodara 'Glacier Blue'

Cedrus deodara 'Gold Cone'

spreads 2 to 4 ft. (0.6 to 1.2 m), golden foliage in full sun, often listed as 'Gold Horizon'.

'Karl Fuchs': more cold hardy and narrower than species, very blue. See photo on pages 10 and 49.

'Kashmir': like the species in habit but more cold-hardy, foliage silver blue-green.

'Pygmy': extremely slow-growing dwarf, less than $2/3$ in. (1.7 cm) a year, useful for trough gardens, blue-green needles $1/2$ in. (1.2 cm) long, also called 'Pygmaea'.

'Raywood's Prostrate Dwarf': vigorous groundcover with blue needles.

'Roman Gold': dense bright golden yellow foliage, sometimes incorrectly listed as 'Wells Golden'.

'Shalimar': soft blue color and graceful habit, upright tree form, selected for hardiness. See photo on page 49.

Cedrus deodara 'Raywood's Prostrate Dwarf'

Cedrus deodara 'Golden Horizon'

Cedrus deodara foliage

Cedrus deodara 'Roman Gold'

Cedrus deodara 'Snow Sprite'

Three selections of *Cedrus deodara*: 'Aurea' (left), 'Karl Fuchs' (center), and 'Shalimar' (right)

'Snow Sprite': creamy white to yellow new growth, small and mounding, eventually forms a leader, give it some shade.

Cedrus libani
Cedar of Lebanon

Zones 5 to 7

The cedar of Lebanon is native to Lebanon, Syria, and the western side of the Taurus Mountains in southern Turkey. It was cultivated in Europe by the 17th century and was planted all across England to commemorate Napoleon's defeat at the battle of Waterloo in 1815. Hence, many great English manors have a cedar of Lebanon that is more than 200 years old.

The tree is stiffly pyramidal in youth but develops a stately flat-topped crown in maturity. It slowly reaches 50 to 60 ft (15 to 18 m) tall in cultivation and 125 ft (38 m) in the wild. The trunk can be massive and is usually multi-stemmed. The foliage is typically held on large branches that grow outward almost horizontally. The needles are arranged alternately and typically appear in rosettes of 10 to 20 until, after two to three years, they are in whorls of 30 to 60 needles per spur, $3/4$ to 1 in. (2 to 2.5 cm) long. The needles are four-sided, stiff, and dark green to gray-green in color. The needles have white lines on all four sides and are pointed. They are borne for only two growing seasons.

The upright yellow pollen-bearing cones appear in autumn on the end of short shoots. They are erect, up to 2 in. (5 cm) long, with yellow pollen. They shed their pollen in early autumn. The immature seed-bearing cones are cylindrical, green, ¾ in. (2 cm) long also at the end of short shoots. The mature cones are held upright. They are single, 3 to 5 in. (7.5 to 12 cm) long, and stalked. The apex of each cone is flat or slightly depressed. They mature the first autumn and break apart over the next year to release the seeds and bract scales. A spiky stalk remains on the shoot. The bark is dark gray or brown and smooth on young trees but becomes black with a pebblelike appearance with maturity.

This cedar should be grown in an open, sunny location in loose, well-drained, acid soil. It grows in clay soil if the drainage is adequate. It has a shallow root system and should not be mulched with alkaline materials like maple leaves or wood ashes. It does not appreciate pollution.

The cedar of Lebanon needs to be 50 years old to look its best. It is a tree for the large property.

Cedrus libani 'Blue Angel'

It could be maintained on a small property by root pruning to restrict its size.

The timber is light, durable, and fragrant. It has been used for centuries for building. King Solomon's temple was said to be constructed from this wood 3000 years ago.

'Blue Angel': narrower than the species with large powder blue needles, reaches 12 ft. (3.5 m) tall by 4 ft. (1.2 m) wide in ten years.

'Brevifolia': not as tall as the species with short needles.

'Glauca Pendula': pendulous habit with distinctly blue needles.

'Green Prince': slow-growing, 1 in. (2.5 cm) a year, deep green dwarf that becomes an open-branched pyramid giving the appearance of great age, excellent choice for trough gardens or bonsai.

Subsp. *stenocoma*: a hardier form that grows in higher elevations throughout the native range of *C. libani*, strong horizontal branching habit, a tough plant, zone 5.

Cedrus libani subsp. *stenocoma*

Cephalotaxus harringtonia
Japanese plum-yew
Zones 6 to 9

Japanese plum-yew is one of a half-dozen or more species in the genus *Cephalotaxus* (plum-yew), all from Korea, China, and Japan. Only a few of the species are hardy enough to be commonly found in gardens.

On first glance, species of *Cephalotaxus* look like their relatives in the genus *Taxus* (common yews), but plum-yews are much larger-leaved, have completely different cones, and are perhaps not so versatile. Despite these differences, plum-yews are eminently garden-worthy plants, and cultivars of *C. harringtonia* are becoming more commonly available.

Japanese plum-yew grows in sun or part shade but typically grows best as an understory shrub. It has the huge advantage to the home gardener of not being so palatable to hoofed browsers as yews famously are. Japanese plum-yew tends to tolerate wetter soils than yews.

Very variable in form, *Cephalotaxus harringtonia* can be a large bush or a small tree. The branches are arranged opposite or in whorls. Some specimens have either pollen-bearing or seed-bearing cones, others have both kinds.

Japanese plum-yews tolerate shearing well and are remarkably heat-tolerant. The cultivars can be grown as specimens in a mixed border, as foundation plantings, or, in the case of *Cephalotaxus harringtonia* 'Fastigiata', in a formal setting.

Variety *drupacea* 'Duke Gardens': a dense, spreading, shade-tolerant shrub with glossy dark green needles whorled around the stem, ascending branches give it a more upright form than 'Prostrata', equally slow-growing, reaches 2 to 3 ft. (0.6 to 0.9 m) tall and wide, female.

Cephalotaxus harringtonia var. *drupacea* 'Duke Gardens'

'Fastigiata': a markedly upright, slow growing form, eventually distinctly vase-shaped, can reach 16 ft. (5 m) tall but usually less than 10 ft. (3 m), with deep green, almost black-green, 1½ to 2½ in. (3.5 to 6 cm) long needles arranged spirally around the stem and facing upward, can be difficult to place, but works well in a formal setting or at an "inside" corner of a structure, male.

'Korean Gold': a fastigiate form, with new growth appearing yellow, then turning pale green, and green with season's end, foliage in whorls, should be protected from winter winds.

Cephalotaxus harringtonia 'Fastigiata'

Cephalotaxus harringtonia 'Korean Gold'

Cephalotaxus harringtonia 'Prostrata' seed-bearing cones

Cephalotaxus harringtonia 'Prostrata'

'**Prostrata**': a low-growing form with spreading branches, 2 to 3 ft. (0.6 to 0.9 m) high and wide, leaves arranged more or less opposite, 1 1/2 to 3 in. (3.5 to 7.5 cm) long, deep dark green with two gray-green bands on the underside displayed in ranks on each side of the stem, pollen-bearing cones are borne hanging under the stem at the leaf axils, nutmeg-shaped seed-bearing cones are about 1 in. (2.5 cm) long, hanging on drooping stalks, maturing over two years from a pale green to a light plum color.

CHAMAECYPARIS
Falsecypress

Although it comprises many of our mainstay garden conifers with all possible shapes, sizes, and foliage variants, this genus is rather small, with only about a half-dozen species. Three are native to North America, one in the east and two in the west, and three are found in eastern Asia. In their native stands these trees are characteristically found in closely packed growths in moist forests.

Many falsecypresses are slow-growing and therefore useful in mixed borders. In addition, countless genuinely dwarf cultivars are available to fill practically any landscape requirement one could think of. The many established nursery selections (with names like 'Compacta', 'Nana', or 'Minima' in various combinations with 'Aurea' or 'Variegata' and the like) have developed from similar source species plants and are only relatively stable. The distinctions among them are often rather subjective, some would say capricious.

Description
The foliage can be juvenile (needlelike) or adult (scalelike, often in flat sprays). Pollen- and seed-bearing cones are on the same tree. The former are barely visible but usually yellow; the latter are round with 6 to 12 shieldlike cone scales (they look like exploding soccer balls) that mature the first year (except *Chamaecyparis nootkatensis*).

ID Features
It is easy to confuse *Chamaecyparis* with *Thuja* (arborvitae), but the most obvious difference is the cones: those of falsecypress are spherical (like a soccer ball), while those of arborvitae are oblong (like a rosebud).

Cultivation
Falsecypresses generally prefer moist, well-drained soil. They commonly appreciate shielding from harsh winds early on. Plants are generally container-grown by nurseries and are easily transplanted.

Uses
Falsecypresses have traditionally been valued for their fragrant, cedarlike wood, which was widely utilized by the First Nations people and later exploited by the colonists.

Chamaecyparis lawsoniana
Lawson falsecypress, Port-Orford-cedar
Zones 5 to 7
Native from southern Oregon to northern California at lower elevations than *Chamaecyparis nootkatensis*, *C. lawsoniana* should be grown

Chamaecyparis lawsoniana

in full sun in cool, moist soil similar to its native habitat along the Pacific Coast. It is a pyramidal tree with horizontal spreading branches that often droop. In native stands it grows to 180 ft. (55 m) tall but in cultivation it usually reaches no more than 60 ft. (18 m).

The foliage is scalelike, in flat fanlike sprays with a blue cast. There are faint white marks on the underside. The foliage is often pendulous at the tips. Some say it smells like parsley. The pollen-bearing cones are bright red in the spring. The seed-bearing cones are $2/3$ in. (0.8 cm) round, maturing from blue-green to a reddish brown. A projection from the cone scale is reflexed. The cones mature the first year but are often retained on the tree. The very thick 6 to 10 in. (15 to 25 cm) bark is silvery brown to red-brown and is deeply ridged and furrowed in maturity. The trunk has a flaring base.

Chamaecyparis lawsoniana can live more than a hundred years. It is used as a specimen in gardens but also can be made into a hedge or screen. It tolerates some shade. It does not sprout from old wood; therefore it must be pruned cautiously if being trained into hedging.

Selections are available with blue, green, and even gold foliage. The numerous dwarf cultivars are particularly favored in British gardens. All the selections prefer moist, well-drained soil and safeguarding from prolonged heat and drought for best growth. Generally speaking these selections are relatively stable and do not revert to the species forms. In the main the variegated gold and white forms should be given some protection from harsh winter sun and winds, although the gold color usually is most prominent in sunny situations. Forms with bluish or plain green foliage are typically hardier and they tolerate some shade.

The wood has been used for everything from household items to posts and boat construction. Nearly all the old-growth forests have been logged.

A serious problem for *Chamaecyparis lawsoniana* is a root disease caused by the fungus *Phytophthora lateralis*. Other (Asian) *Chamaecyparis* species and *C. nootkatensis* seem to be resistant. Losses from this disease have been severe in the Pacific Northwest especially along water courses and rural roads. The disease enters in the rootlets and spreads through the inner bark and cambium. The infected tissue dies and effectively girdles the tree. Later the foliage is affected and withers. The disease is spread through earth movement by construction and logging opera-

Chamaecyparis lawsoniana seed-bearing cones

Chamaecyparis lawsoniana 'Green Globe'

Chamaecyparis lawsoniana 'Oregon Blue'

Chamaecyparis lawsoniana 'Pembury Blue'

tions as well as along moving water. The fungus also moves on the feet of domestic and wild animals. Many cultivars have disappeared from the nursery trade because of losses, and many mature trees have had to be replaced with other species. *Chamaecyparis lawsoniana* can still be enjoyed in low-risk sites with attention to minimizing introduction of the disease. Genetically resistant stock has not been developed.

'**Alumnii**': columnar tree to 25 ft. (8 m) tall with densely ascending branches, soft-textured gray-blue adult foliage in flat sprays.

'**Green Globe**': a dense rounded compact dwarf eventually reaching 1 to 2 ft. (0.3 to 0.6 m) tall, perfect for rock or trough gardens.

'**Oregon Blue**': a broad column with outstanding silver-blue foliage, drooping branch tips, grows fast, reaching 50 ft. (15 m) tall.

'**Pelt's Blue**': a tight narrow column 15 to 20 ft. (4.5 to 6 m) high with intense blue foliage in dense flat sprays, good for an accent or hedging.

'**Pembury Blue**': perhaps the best bright silver-blue foliage held in upright vertical sprays, in a 25 to 50 ft. (8 to 15 m) column.

'Schneeball': a white variegated globose dwarf.

'Silver Threads': a narrow pyramidal dwarf with creamy variegation.

'Stardust': upright and vigorous with clear yellow foliage throughout.

'Yvonne': upright conical shape with bright golden yellow foliage, reaches 3 ft. (0.9 m) tall.

Chamaecyparis nootkatensis
Alaska-cedar
Zones 4 to 7

Also called Nootka-cypress, Nootka falsecypress, yellow-cypress, and yellow-cedar, this species is found from Alaska south to British Columbia and south along the Cascade Mountains to northern California. In its native habitat, it reaches the greatest size, up to 150 ft. (46 m) tall. Considering that annual precipitation in its wild habitat exceeds 60 in. (150 cm), it is no revelation that this plant demands plenty of moisture. It tolerates some shade. It is a slow-growing species and can live 2000 years or more. In cultivation it is faster growing and displays denser foliage.

The tree has a weeping habit with the secondary branchlets draped toward the ground from the principal branches, which sweep in a graceful upward curve. Typically the tree's leading shoot droops. The dark blue-green foliage is in flat sprays. The foliage can feel prickly to the touch because the scalelike leaves are sharply pointed. There are no white markings on the underside. The foliage emits an unpleasant resinous odor when crushed. To some observers it smells like a cut potato.

The pollen-bearing cones are yellow and on side branches of the previous year's growth. They are shed in early spring. The 1/2 in. (1.2 cm) thick seed-bearing cones are found near the tips of branchlets and are red-brown, maturing during the second year. Each scale has a noticeable horny point. These scales separate and release the seeds when mature.

The young bark is scaly and with maturity becomes gray with narrow intersecting ridges. The bark does not peel off in long strips as does that of *Thuja plicata*, a species sometimes confused with this one. The tree trunk is buttressed at the base. The bark is only 1/2 in. (1.2 cm) thick and provides no protection from fires, though these are not common in the moist areas this tree inhabits. The tree carries snow loads well.

Chamaecyparis nootkatensis is propagated by cuttings generally. When grafted it does not "take" onto *Chamaecyparis* but is successful on *Cupressus* or *Thuja orientalis*. It is one of the par-

Chamaecyparis lawsoniana 'Schneeball'

Chamaecyparis nootkatensis foliage and seed-bearing cones

ents of the intergeneric hybrid ×*Cupressocyparis leylandii*.

Like various other conifers, the North American *Chamaecyparis nootkatensis* bears the common name cedar because *Chamaecyparis* was unknown to the arriving colonists, and the fragrant wood evidently reminded them of the familiar *Cedrus*. The wood was favored by the First Nations peoples for boat construction, long house construction, and totems. It is strong despite being light in weight and is very durable when exposed to moisture. This is a tree to celebrate in the larger landscape; there are only a few selections for the mixed border.

'Aurea': pyramidal, slower growing and denser than the species, foliage is yellow in youth, later becoming more yellow-green.

'Green Arrow': a narrow form with branches that sweep straight downward close to the trunk, often forming a skirt at the base, could be planted in groups to cause a commotion.

'Jubilee': very narrow and fast-growing with descending branches of rich green foliage, more narrowly weeping than 'Pendula'.

Chamaecyparis nootkatensis 'Green Arrow'

Chamaecyparis nootkatensis 'Pendula'

CHAMAECYPARIS NOOTKATENSIS

'**Pendula**': an elegant weeping tree with pendulous secondary branches, two forms in cultivation, one slender and dense, the other fuller with widely spaced sweeping branches.

'**Strict Weeper**': more narrowly weeping than 'Pendula', also listed as 'Strict Weeping'.

'**Van den Akker**': one of the narrowest forms. Striking.

'**Variegata**': habit like the species but blue-green foliage is speckled with white.

Chamaecyparis nootkatensis 'Variegata' foliage

Chamaecyparis nootkatensis 'Strict Weeper'

Another form of *Chamaecyparis nootkatensis* 'Pendula'

Chamaecyparis obtusa
Hinoki falsecypress
Zones 5 to 8

The hinoki falsecypress is native to Japan, where it is an important timber tree and is considered sacred by Shintos. It develops into a large, broad, and conical tree, 125 ft. (38 m) tall in the wild and 50 to 75 ft. (15 to 23 m) tall in cultivation. This species is rather more adaptable to heat and drought conditions than its cousins.

The foliage, a rich dark green, is held in short flat sprays. The leaves are bluntly rounded at the tips (hence *obtusa*—sometimes the Latin names are helpful!), and there are white X-shaped markings on the undersurface. The solitary, rounded, seed-bearing cones are held on short stalks. They mature to an orange-brown color the first year. The bark at maturity is a bright red-brown, furrowed and peeling off in long, thin strips.

Chamaecyparis obtusa showing the white marking on the leaf underside and the "exploding soccer ball" seed-bearing cones

Chamaecyparis obtusa cultivars are popular in mixed borders

Like the Lawson falsecypress, the hinoki falsecypress is more apt to be seen in arboreta and large landscapes. However, there are myriad cultivars to satisfy every imaginable need of the home gardener and landscape designer, many of them challenging to differentiate from one another. No Asian-style garden would be authentic without the inclusion of this species, and it is a favorite (dare I say darling?) of bonsai enthusiasts (see photo on page 000). Many of the slow-growing selections are good choices for container culture.

'Compacta': dense and broadly conical, reaching 16 ft. (5 m) tall.

'Coralliformis': dwarf and bushy mound with unique dark green, twisted, cordlike foliage, reaches 5 ft. (1.5 m) tall after 25 years.

'Crippsii': slow-growing, wide-spreading branches with drooping tips, golden yellow, ferny frond foliage with good winter color, broadly conical to 15 ft. (4.5 m) tall by 8 ft. (2.5 m) wide. A choice accent plant.

'Elmwood Gold': bright yellow in summer, bronze in winter, reaches 4 ft. (1.2 m) tall by 3 ft. (0.9 m) wide in ten years.

Chamaecyparis obtusa 'Crippsii' foliage

Chamaecyparis obtusa 'Coralliformis'

Chamaecyparis obtusa 'Elmwood Gold'

'**Fernspray Gold**': slender and slow-growing, reaches 10 ft. (3 m) tall after many years, bright yellow foliage all year, useful as an accent, can be sheared, benefits from wind protection.

'**Filicoides**': a small open-growing bush with long thin branches and flat fernlike foliage, in time reaching 5 ft. (1.5 m) tall.

'**Gracilis**': dense dark green foliage in shell-shaped sprays, the branch tips droop, pyramidal form can reach 40 ft. (12 m) tall.

'**Green Cushion**': a very dwarf bun.

'**Intermedia**': a flat-topped rounded form with light green dense foliage, grows slowly to 1 ft. (0.3 m) tall, useful for trough gardens.

'**Jean Iseli**': a miniature mound with deep green compact foliage.

'**Kamakurahiba**': a dwarf, low-growing, graceful shrub with cock's-comblike branchlets tipped yellow-white.

'**Kosteri**': an upright bushy form with bright green, twisting, mossy foliage that bronzes in winter, eventually reaches 5 ft. (1.5 m) tall by 4 ft. (1.2 m) wide, appreciates protection from drought and harsh winds, a favorite of gardeners.

'**Little Marky**': a dense pyramidal dwarf with chartreuse-yellow foliage, reaches 30 in. (75 cm) tall in 15 years.

Chamaecyparis obtusa 'Green Cushion'

Chamaecyparis obtusa 'Little Marky'

Chamaecyparis obtusa 'Jean Iseli'

'**Meroke Twin**': a pillar-shaped dwarf with bright lemon-yellow foliage that turns deep gold, reaches 3 to 6 ft. (0.9 to 1.8 m) tall.

'**Minima**': a very slow growing tight bun, can take ten years to reach 6 in. (15 cm) tall.

'**Nana Aurea**': bright yellow cupped sprays of foliage, to 6 ft. (1.8 m) tall by 3 ft. (0.9 m) wide.

'**Nana Gracilis**': glossy dark green dense cupped foliage, conical when mature, reaching 3 ft. (0.9 m) tall, a universally admired cultivar that has been cultivated in gardens for more than a century.

'**Opaal**': similar to 'Nana Gracilis' but foliage yellow-green, produces cones when young.

'**Pygmaea**': a rounded, wide-spreading form with flat, fan-shaped glossy-green foliage, purple-tinged in winter, name not exactly appropriate since the plant can reach 6 ft. (1.8 m) tall.

'**Reis Dwarf**': fine-textured and bright green with twisted branches that project from the plant creating irregular shapes that are not reversions and should not be pruned.

'**Tempelhof**': broadly cone-shaped with dense olive-green fan-shaped foliage and orangish stems.

Chamaecyparis obtusa 'Minima'

Chamaecyparis obtusa 'Nana Gracilis' in a container

Chamaecyparis obtusa 'Opaal'

Chamaecyparis pisifera
Sawara-cypress
Zones 4 to 8

The sawara-cypress is native to Japan's southern islands of Honshu and Kyushu, where it is an important timber tree. In its native habitat it can reach 150 ft. (46 m) tall, but in cultivation it is usually half that size. It is more likely to be found in arboreta than home landscapes. This species varies a great deal, from the large native trees to tiny garden selections with foliage in all shades of green, blue, yellow, white, and variegated.

The foliage is scalelike, in flat sprays, with incurved tips. The leaves are sharply pointed and have white markings below. The Latin *pisifera* ("pea bearing") refers to the tiny, round, spiny cones, which are carried within the foliage or slightly beneath it. They mature in the first year. However, this species does not produce cones

Chamaecyparis pisifera

freely. The bark is smooth, dark red-brown, and peels in long narrow strips.

Many cultivars of this species have "normal" foliage, but lots of the selections available for garden use are quite different from the type in personality, form, and appearance. For unclear reasons, cultivars of this species have (Latinized) group names. Sorting out the nomenclature of some of these plants is difficult. The Squarrosa Group has only juvenile foliage with soft, needlelike leaves. Often blue-toned, the plants have a fluffy appearance. Examples are 'Squarrosa Intermedia' and 'Boulevard'. The Plumosa Group has part juvenile foliage with needlelike foliage or persistent semi-juvenile foliage ('Plumosa Aurea' and 'Snow', for example). The awl-shaped leaves stand out at a 45° angle to the stem and are soft. Filifera Group selections have whiplike foliage; examples are 'Filifera Aurea', 'Golden Mop', 'Sungold', and 'Gold Spangle'. No white markings are detectable.

Chamaecyparis pisifera 'Boulevard' poodled

'Boulevard': a dense conical habit with soft silver-blue juvenile foliage, becomes purple-tinged in winter, usually develops patches of dead foliage which must be trimmed out and does not look good unless sheared into a bun or poodled, useful in containers, withstands heavy pruning.

'Curly Tops': similar to 'Boulevard' but lateral shoots are twisted and curled, juvenile leaves are glaucous blue with white bands, persistent interior brown needles, rounded habit, reaches 6 ft. (1.8 m) tall.

'Filifera': dense and broadly pyramidal, finely textured stringlike sprays of green foliage draped on whiplike pendulous branches, reaches 6 to 8 ft. (1.8 to 2.5 m) tall and up to 15 ft. (4.5 m) wide, easy to grow, adds a delicate look to a border.

'Filifera Aurea': like 'Filifera' in form but with golden yellow foliage that is maintained year-round if not shaded, shape and size can be con-

Chamaecyparis pisifera 'Filifera Aurea'

trolled by pruning, a great contrast in the winter landscape.

'Filifera Aureovariegata': whiplike branches are splashed with yellow, slower growing than 'Filifera Aurea', very showy.

'Gold Spangle': bright yellow, threadlike foliage with some sections more congested, broadly pyramidal habit, fast-growing to 7 ft. (2 m) tall by 3 ft. (0.9 m) wide, needs protectection from harsh sun.

Chamaecyparis pisifera 'Gold Spangle'

'Golden Mop': a low and mounding dwarf with bright golden finely threadlike foliage, slow to establish, requires protection from harsh sun, also listed as 'Filifera Golden Mops'.

'Lemon Thread': fine-textured rich gold foliage, fast-growing to 20 ft. (6 m) tall and wide.

'Snow': mossy, blue-gray, ferny, semi-juvenile foliage, whiter at tips of new growth, vigorous and dense, reaches 6 ft. (1.8 m) tall unless pruned.

'Sungold': dwarf and mounding, threadlike foliage with gold new growth, turning green in winter, vigorous, does not need protection from sun.

'White Pygmy': white feathery new growth with green within, forms a flat globe only 3 ft. (7.6 m) tall by 12 in. (30.5 cm) wide after ten years, good choice for rock gardens.

Chamaecyparis pisifera 'Golden Mop'

Chamaecyparis pisifera 'Lemon Thread'

Chamaecyparis pisifera 'Sungold' foliage

Chamaecyparis pisifera 'White Pygmy'

Cryptomeria japonica
Japanese-cedar
Zone 5

Cryptomeria japonica is native to and planted throughout Japan, where it is very important both as an ornamental plant and as a source of wood. It is the only species in its genus and can grow to 160 ft. (49 m) tall. Japanese-cedars are the oldest and largest living trees of Japan. More than 200 cultivars are known, including many dwarf forms.

Cryptomerias are valuable in the designed landscape because of their graceful habit, shade tolerance, and beautiful foliage. They appreciate well-drained, moist soil, and protection from harsh winter winds. The trees can be sheared (they even grow from the stump if cut off) and are not prone to any common pests or diseases.

Most of the cryptomerias available were selected in Japan. "Sugi" is the Japanese common name for the species and is often part of the name of numerous cultivars that were introduced prior to 1959.

In youth cryptomerias are cone-shaped, but with age they open out and spaces appear among the branches, giving them a poodled look. They usually have a pointed or sometimes broadly domed top. The foliage is needlelike, soft, dark green, surrounding the stem, and awl-shaped ("keeled"). The base of the needle clasps the stem; the needle itself diverges from the shoot and points toward the growing tip. The stem of the new growth is green. Many forms change color in the winter, commonly varying from a light bronze to a deep purple, but then quickly green up again in spring.

Japanese-cedar is monoecious. The pollen-bearing cones appear in spring in the axils of the leaves and are yellow-green in clusters of 20 or more, at the ends of branchlets. The immature seed-bearing cones are globular and solitary at the ends of branchlets. The mature seed-bearing cones are round and prickly, green when immature and maturing to brown in one season. They are at the ends of shoots and remain on the tree for months even after shedding their seeds. The bark is red-brown, fibrous, and soft. With maturity the bark peels off in long strips. The trunk is usually straight, sometimes buttressed at the base.

Leaf blight, a fungus disorder, can cause interior foliage to turn brown and unsightly. Fungicide sprays can be applied. It is best to avoid the problem by providing good air circulation and planting specimens where they get the drying morning sun.

The timber is economically important in Japan. The wood is very rot-resistant and easily worked; it is used for buildings, bridges, ships, posts, and pulp. Cryptomerias are often planted around temples.

'Bandai-sugi': slow-growing, globose habit, dense bright green mosslike foliage turning deep bronze in winter, irregular growth with some branchlets growing strongly, others are short, reaches 4 ft. (1.2 m) tall in ten years.

'Barabits' Gold': indistinguishable from 'Sekkan-sugi'.

'Benjamin Franklin': vigorous upright habit, foliage remains green during the winter, salt-tolerant, reaches 20 ft (6 m) tall.

'Black Dragon': vigorous, dense, upright conical habit to 6 ft. (1.8 m) tall, pale green spring growth ages to deep dark green, which is retained in winter.

Cryptomeria japonica cones: mature seed-bearing cones are round, brown, and prickly; pollen-bearing cones are yellow-green in clusters at the ends of branchlets.

Cryptomeria japonica 'Cristata' foliage

Cryptomeria japonica 'Elegans Nana' winter color

Cryptomeria japonica 'Globosa Nana'

'Cristata': slow-growing narrow bush or small tree with ascending branches, branch tips appear as if pasted together, giving a twisted, deformed look, reaches 10 ft. (3 m) tall, can be pruned to call attention to the cock's-comblike branchlets.

'Elegans Nana': compact globe to cloud-shaped, slow-growing to 3 to 4 ft. (0.9 to 1.2 m) tall, soft billowy blue-green foliage turning purple-brown in winter, needs protection from winter sun and wind.

'Globosa Nana': broadly rounded, 3 to 4 ft. (0.9 to 1.2 m) tall and wide, pendulous branchlets, deep green foliage with tightly pressed needles, bronzes in winter, needs protection from winter sun and wind.

'Gyokuryu': irregular globe to 3 ft. (0.9 m) tall and wide, dark green foliage turning bronze in winter, should be protected from winter wind.

'Knaptonensis': slow-growing, upright and mounding, creamy white new growth, prefers some shade and wind protection.

'Koshyi': spreading habit, reaching 6 in. (15 cm) tall by 20 in. (50 cm) wide in 20 years, pale green foliage, needs protection from afternoon sun and winter wind.

'Rein's Dense Jade': formal-looking with jade-green closely appressed needles, bronzes in winter.

'Sekkan-sugi': dense, upright to 30 ft. (9 m) tall, foliage cream to bright yellow-gold tipped in summer, less in winter, needs protection from drying winds and full sun.

Cryptomeria japonica 'Rein's Dense Jade'

Cryptomeria japonica 'Sekkan-sugi'

'Spiralis': broad and pyramidal, foliage pressed against stem so tightly that the stems appear twisted like yarn, bright green year-round, benefits from shaping.

Cryptomeria japonica 'Spiralis' foliage

Cryptomeria japonica 'Tansu'

Cryptomeria japonica 'Spiraliter Falcata'

CRYPTOMERIA JAPONICA

'Spiraliter Falcata': more dwarf and upright than 'Spiralis', branches twist and curve and are thinner.

'Tansu': small and rounded with dense light green foliage, bronzes in winter, grows 2 to 3 in. (5 to 7.5 cm) a year, reaching 2 ft. (0.6 m) tall, good for bonsai and rock gardens.

'Vilmorin Gold': rounded habit with yellow-gold foliage in summer.

'Vilmoriniana': very slow-growing to 20 in. (50 cm) tall in ten years, dense, deep green short needles that bronze in winter, good for trough gardens.

'Yoshino': beautiful pyramidal form reaching 20 ft. (6 m) tall by 8 ft. (2.5 m) wide, growing 1 ft. (0.3 m) a year, rich green foliage year-round, retains branches to ground, does well in the shade. Choice. A good replacement for *Tsuga*.

Cryptomeria japonica 'Yoshino'

Cunninghamia lanceolata
China-fir

Zones 6 to 9

This species is a forest tree of China, where it is valued for its timber. It is not actually a fir or even in the same family as the true firs (*Abies*). The tree grows to 75 ft. (23 m) tall and 30 ft. (9 m) wide with a single stem. The habit is often broadly pyramidal with a rounded top. The branches are usually widely spaced and somewhat drooping.

The bright glossy green needles are lance-shaped (hence its epithet), 1 to 2½ in. (2.5 to 6 cm) long. They are very flexible but have a wickedly sharp tip. They are usually displayed in two ranks, often curving upward a bit. There are two white bands beneath. The pollen-bearing cones are small and in terminal clusters (occasionally at the base of seed cones), through which the new shoots grow. The ovoid seed-bearing cones are green, maturing to brown; they are solitary and terminal. The attractive bark is cinnamon-brown and hard, peeling off in long irregular strips.

Cunninghamia lanceolata suckers from the base and can be grown as a shrub by pruning. It does best in areas of mild winters and appreciates plentiful moisture. It is adaptable to a wide range of soils and withstands salt spray but should be given protection from harsh winds.

This species is not practical for the home landscape but can be found in most arboretum collections. It is a bit of a horticultural oddity. Old specimens often look rather ragged. The needles fall while still attached to large twigs, thus it is usually covered with conspicuous clumps of dead foliage that likewise litter the ground under it. These dead needles are very flammable.

The wood is soft but durable, easily worked, and resistant to rot. It is used for general construction, bridges, ships, posts, furniture, and coffins.

'Chanson's Gift': neater than the species, single-stemmed, more compact and pyramidal, with glossy darker green foliage.

'Glauca': more silvery blue new foliage and often has a pendulous habit, considered hardier

Cunninghamia lanceolata seed-bearing cones and foliage

Cunninghamia lanceolata 'Glauca'

than the species and makes a very attractive specimen when well grown, best to clip to encourage new growth.

'Little Leo': a cushion-shaped plant with short leaves, needs some shelter, grows 1½ in. (3.5 cm) a year.

×*Cupressocyparis leylandii*
Leyland cypress
Zones 6 to 10

The Leyland cypress is a versatile and adaptable conifer that combines the rapid growth of its Monterey cypress (*Cupressus macrocarpa*) parent and the hardiness and habit of its Alaska-cedar (*Chamaecyparis nootkatensis*) parent. It is a very attractive tree with a dense columnar habit, and it grows much faster than either parent, 2 to 4 ft. (0.6 to 1.2 m) a year, to a height of 60 ft. (18 m).

This cypress tolerates coastal conditions and most soils, and is said to withstand salt better than any other conifer. Give it full sun, or it will be less vigorous. It is very pollution-tolerant.

The soft foliage is carried in flat sprays that radiate in all directions from the stem and are slightly drooping. The foliage color is held during the winter. Cones are said to be common on most selections, but, in fact, are hard to find. They are ½ in. (1.2 cm) round, with shieldlike scales and a small spine. The mature bark is dark brown with shallow ridges.

The numerous selections of ×*Cupressocyparis leylandii* make handsome, fine-textured specimens. The Leyland cypress has become especially valued in England because it withstands trimming and thus has become a common conifer for hedging. It is unequaled for tall screens but can quickly outgrow its space in residential landscapes. It is widely grown as a holiday tree, although it is not fragrant and the branches do not hold ornaments well.

The Leyland cypress does not set seed and must be propagated by cuttings. It is best container-grown. In areas with cold winters the best success with this species is by buying small, container-grown specimens and planting them in the spring. This allows the plants to distribute their fibrous roots in the gardener's soil. Larger specimens planted in the fall in exposed sites are subject to heaving out of frozen soil or being blown over by winds.

The most important disease that affects Leylands is caused by several fungal species of *Seiridium*. Cankers form at damaged bark and resin will be seen; oozing causes dieback of leading shoots. Bagworms (see the discussion at *Thuja*) can be a problem also.

'Gold Rider': fast-growing with a narrow crown, to 70 ft. (21 m) tall by 12 ft. (3.6 m) wide, golden foliage not burned by sun.

×*Cupressocyparis leylandii* 'Gold Rider'

×*CUPRESSOCYPARIS LEYLANDII*

'**Green Spire**': narrow and columnar with dense, bright green foliage.

'**Harlequin**': foliage has creamy white patches, similar to 'Silver Dust'.

×*Cupressocyparis leylandii* 'Harlequin' foliage

×*Cupressocyparis leylandii* 'Silver Dust'

×*Cupressocyparis leylandii* 'Naylor's Blue'

'Naylor's Blue': vigorous, tall columnar form to 50 ft. (15 m) tall with open branching, gray-blue foliage turns bluer in cold weather, requires good drainage and protection from wind.

'Silver Dust': columnar tree with creamy white variegation.

'Star Wars': tall and pyramidal, dense foliage with uniform white variegation.

CUPRESSUS
Cypress

The trees or large shrubs comprising this genus grow in North America (mainly California, Mexico, and Central America), southern Europe, Africa, and Asia. Many of the cypresses occur in small isolated stands. Authorities cannot agree on the classification of plants in this genus; some of the 13 to 25 present species have been moved back and forth between *Cupressus* (true cypress) and *Chamaecyparis* (falsecypress).

Cupressus has been cultivated for thousands of years in the Mediterranean region and near Buddhist temples in China, Tibet, and India. It is admired in public gardens and arboreta in the West.

Description

The foliage is scalelike, and in many species has resinous glands that are aromatic and sticky when crushed. Cones appear on the tips of shoots. The pollen-bearing cones are evident in late winter. The seed-bearing cones usually mature in two years and are round and woody with projections on the surface. The cones can remain on the tree for years. The seeds are sometimes not released until opened by fire.

ID Features

Cupressus may be distinguished from *Chamaecyparis* by the generally larger cones and lesser cold hardiness.

Cultivation

Cypresses grow best in full sun. The plants are tolerant of almost any soil condition that is not constantly wet. They are considered difficult to transplant and should be purchased container-grown.

Uses

The wood is prized for its sweet scent and resistance to decay.

Cupressus arizonica
Arizona cypress
Zones 7 to 9

Given that the Arizona cypress is native to southwestern Arizona, New Mexico, and Mexico, it obviously tolerates hot, dry conditions and should be grown in full sun. It is a small to medium-sized tree 40 to 50 ft. (12 to 15 m) tall and half as wide with a broadly columnar rounded crown. The dense foliage is scalelike, pointed, and blue-green. The cones are 1¼ in. (3 cm) round with pointed scales. The bark is red-brown and peeling.

The species is not often found in gardens, but selections from its several varieties, notably var. *glabra* (smooth cypress), are valued. Over the species as a whole there is intergradation between smooth and fibrous barks, and these variations of bark texture as well as foliage features have been used by some authorities to segregate additional species. Some of the following cultivars are no doubt actually selections of var. *glabra* (and could even be listed as *Cupressus glabra*: some authorities consider *C. arizonica* and *C. glabra* synonymous). Regardless of their specific epithet, a single plant of many of these cultivars makes a

Cupressus arizonica cone

Cupressus arizonica 'Blue Ice'

dramatic statement in the garden. They are very popular in Australia and New Zealand.

'Arctic': upright and pyramidal with horizontal branching, rich green foliage with white tips early in the season, slow-growing to 20 ft. (6 m) tall.

'Blue Ice': upright habit, frosty blue-gray foliage, showy red-brown stems, slow growing to 15 ft. (4.5 m) tall, wind-tolerant.

'Blue Pyramid': compact, symmetrical, and pyramidal habit, silver-gray foliage, reaches 20 to 25 ft. (6 to 8 m) tall.

'Golden Pyramid': gold-tinted foliage, strong grower, 15 ft. (4.5 m) tall by 5 ft. (1.5 m) wide in 15 years.

'Sapphire Skies': narrow and pyramidal with rich blue-green foliage.

Cupressus arizonica 'Sapphire Skies' foliage

Cupressus arizonica 'Blue Pyramid'

Cupressus arizonica 'Golden Pyramid'

Cupressus macrocarpa 'Lutea'

Cupressus macrocarpa
Monterey cypress
Zones 7 to 9

This beautiful tree is found near the Monterey Peninsula of California. Its habit depends on growing conditions. Trees overlooking the Pacific Ocean are densely foliaged, stunted, and irregular in habit, whereas those further from shore are taller and straighter.

The Monterey cypress grows fast and makes a nice hedge plant in areas with a mild and humid climate. It does not tolerate drought. Because of its salt tolerance, it is a good species for growing near the sea.

Under good conditions this cypress grows to 75 ft. (23 m) tall and develops a broad flat crown; it can live for hundreds of years. The dense foliage is a rich bright green and is not resinous. The persistent solitary or sometimes paired cones are 1 to 1$\frac{1}{3}$ in. (2.5 to 3.3 cm) wide, maturing in two years with shieldlike scales. The bark is red-brown and ridged with maturity.

This species is often grown in New Zealand and Australia and is perhaps best known as one of the parents of ×*Cupressocyparis leylandii* (Leyland cypress).

'Aurea': upright, irregularly pyramidal with gold foliage.

'Lutea': narrow and pyramidal with bright yellow new growth that turns green, slow-growing, seed-bearing cones are yellow.

Cupressus sempervirens
Italian cypress
Zones 7 to 9

The Italian cypress is native to the eastern Mediterranean across to Iran. Most common in cultivation is var. *stricta*, the very narrow vertical tree always featured on postcards from Tuscany.

This species grows 60 to 90 ft. (18 to 27 m) in height with a spread of only 8 ft. (2.5 m). It tolerates long hot summers. The leaves are scalelike and dark green in short flat sprays. The pollen-bearing cones are small and yellow. The glossy

Cupressus sempervirens cone

Cupressus sempervirens 'Totem'

brown-gray seed-bearing cones are 1 1/3 in. (3.3 cm) round with little round knobs on the scales. They mature in two years but often persist on the tree.

The species is said to live up to a thousand years and to be tolerant of drought, wind, and dust and not fussy about soil pH. The fragrant wood is moth-repellent, durable, and easily worked.

'**Swane's Gold**': slender compact column, slow-growing to 4 ft. (1.2 m) tall in ten years, ultimately 12 ft. (3.6 m) tall, golden yellow foliage in youth, becoming bronze in winter, ideal for small gardens.

'**Totem**': a very narrow upright column, deep green foliage, reaches 12 ft. (3.6 m) tall by 20 in. (50 cm) wide in ten years, also listed as 'Totem Pole'.

Ginkgo biloba
Maidenhair tree
Zones 4 to 8

The maidenhair tree grows rather slowly at first but can reach 80 ft. (24 m) tall and live for a thousand years. In youth it is rather spare-looking, but it becomes very wide-spreading with maturity.

Except for full sun the tree has few requirements. It is tolerant of urban and industrial conditions and has been widely used as a street tree. Wet sites should be avoided; otherwise, this Chinese native is cultivated in North America from Montreal to New Orleans. It is also free of insect pests and diseases.

The distinctive alternate leaves are fan-shaped, usually two-lobed (that is, with a deep central notch), on spur shoots. They are apple-green on both sides and scalloped along the margins.

Ginkgo biloba

Very fine parallel veins radiate from the base of the leaf. The leaves are clustered three to five on small shoots. Both long and short shoots are produced. The short shoots have leaves in a tight spiral and are covered with circles of leaf scars; each marking a year's growth. There are long shoots with leaves spirally arranged. The foliage turns a clear yellow in the autumn. It has been observed that the leaves all seem to fall at once, carpeting the ground in a circle under the tree. The bark on mature plants is thick, gray-black with shallow fissures.

Ginkgo is dioecious. The pollen-bearing cones are catkinlike in small clusters, pendulous from the spur shoots, and appear in the spring. The "sperm" are motile and depend on water to travel to the seed-bearing cone. Seed-bearing cones, $3/4$ to 1 in. (2 to 2.5 cm) round, develop on the dwarf shoots, usually carrying only one seed. The cones are produced in pairs or threes and mature and fall in autumn the first year.

The seeds (kernels) themselves are smooth and silvery white, covered by a hard shell with a thick fleshy coat, and are a special delicacy roasted in Asian cooking. The seeds are steamed until the shell cracks, then the kernel is removed and eaten or used in baked dishes. They are said to taste like baked potatoes or chestnuts.

Ginkgo takes decades to begin to produce cones. Thus, it can take some time before owners are unhappy to learn they have a female tree, the seed-bearing cones of which smell like carrion when crushed. Putrid. For that reason, male trees should be selected and planted.

The common name arises from the resemblance of the leaf to the maidenhair fern (*Adiantum pedatum*). The tree is regarded as sacred in Asia, where it has been considered a symbol of changelessness, hope, love, protection, and longevity. The topknots worn by samurais and sumo wrestlers are shaped like a ginkgo leaf. The light, fine-grained wood of the tree is of little economic value; it is often used to make tea utensils and chessmen.

Ginkgo biloba cones and fall leaf color

Ginkgo biloba 'Mariken'

'Autumn Gold': upright branching, excellent autumn color, reaches 50 ft. (15 m) tall by 30 ft. (9 m) wide, male.

'Chi-chi': dwarf, dense, multistemmed habit, reaches 4 ft. (1.2 m) tall in ten years, male.

'Mariken': compact with pendulous branches, male.

'Princeton Sentry': columnar fastigiate form, male.

'**Saratoga**': distinctly upright habit, dense ascending branches with distinct central leader, male.

'**Tremonia**': narrowly fastigiate form, large leaves, reaches 30 ft. (9 m) tall, female.

'**Tubifolia**': slow-growing, compact, slender tube-shaped leaves, also listed as 'Tubiformis'.

JUNIPERUS
Juniper

More than 60 species of junipers are found in the Northern Hemisphere. Over a dozen are native to North America. Many are useful in public landscapes and private gardens, some because of their ornamental qualities but most because they are of undemanding cultivation.

The home gardener usually thinks of junipers as providing prostrate and creeping groundcovers in sunny locations, but many selections are shrubby or upright in habit and some are even tall columnar landscape trees. Junipers are widely available and have contributed greatly to the enhancement of gardens the world over.

Many named cultivars lack satisfactory descriptions. Selections of *Juniperus chinensis* (Chinese juniper) may be hybrids with *J. sabina* (savin juniper). Recent analysis recommends that such crosses be listed as *J.* ×*pfitzeriana* (Pfitzer juniper). In Europe, a good number of Pfitzer junipers are listed as cultivars of *J.* ×*media* and in the United States as cultivars of *J. chinensis*. Most of the selections in this group of junipers are groundcovers or spreading and shrub-sized. There appears no handy resolution to this situation, and coniferites will dispute a number of the listings.

Description

Some junipers have sharply pointed needlelike foliage (prickly juvenile) and others have flat and scalelike (smooth adult) foliage that hugs the stem. Many have both types. All young plants bear needlelike leaves. The juvenile foliage is more likely to be retained on the trees that are pruned or grown in thin soil. Juniper foliage can be seen in every shade of green as well as sil-

Ginkgo biloba 'Saratoga'

Ginkgo biloba 'Tubifolia' foliage

ver and yellow. The awl-shaped needles have white bands on the upper inner surface, which sometimes look like they are on the lower side because of the makeup of the branches. Almost all junipers are dioecious, that is, the pollen- and seed-bearing cones appear on different plants. The female plants bear fleshy bluish cones (juniper "berries").

ID Features

The foliage of *Juniperus* is often indistinguishable from that of *Cupressus* (cypress), and identifying and sorting through this genus is difficult even for the trained eye.

Cultivation

Junipers prefer full sun with good drainage, and nearly all are not finicky about soil conditions. They are drought resistant, and often appropriate for tough situations with poor soil and harsh climates. Most are even tolerant of lime. Junipers can withstand shaping and can be developed into hedges.

Pests and Diseases

Many junipers, especially newly transplanted ones, are susceptible to tip blights. The common phomopsis tip blight (*Phomopsis juniperovora*) first presents as yellow spots on young needles but eventually causes dieback of new shoots and entire branches. The fungus infection is spread by splashing rain and wind or by insects and is persistent in dead foliage. Infected twigs and branches should be pruned during dry weather and destroyed. Chemical control is usually not needed. To prevent problems, select resistant cultivars, provide good air circulation, and avoid planting junipers in shaded areas. Junipers are also frequently infested with bagworms (see the discussion at *Thuja*).

Needlelike juniper foliage

Scalelike juniper foliage with fleshy cones ("berries")

Uses

The tastiness of juniper "berries" to birds helps to explain the wide colonization of junipers. Birds especially attracted to junipers include cedar waxwings, robins, and mockingbirds.

Juniperus chinensis
Chinese juniper
Zones 4 to 9

The variability of this native of Japan and China is confounding even to the most authoritative botanists. Some forms of the species can grow to 50 ft. (15 m) tall but most are shrubby or creeping groundcovers. Many exhibit both juvenile foliage with a spiny point borne in sets of two or three and blunt-tipped adult foliage, but numerous named selections have only one type of foliage or the other. The foliage is green to blue-green and gray-green. The pollen- and seed-bearing cones are carried on separate plants. The seed-bearing cones are fleshy and berrylike, violet-brown, and about ½ in. (1.2 cm) in diameter.

Chinese junipers are easy to grow and they tolerate both acid and alkaline soils. They also tolerate light dappled shade but do best in full sun. Those with yellowish foliage require sun. Established plants tolerate dry situations.

Selections of this species are much confused in the trade, often listed as *Juniperus* ×*pfitzeriana* or even *J.* ×*media*. Whatever their name, the 85 or more cultivars are widely grown as ornamentals in North America and Europe. There is a form to satisfy every design requirement, including hedging.

The Chinese junipers are commonly associated with Asian-style gardens, where they are clipped annually into various shapes. They are also popular with bonsai enthusiasts. The wood is used for carving and posts.

'**Aurea**': golden columnar form, dense and narrow, mixture of prickly juvenile and smooth adult foliage, bright color year-round, needs protection from wind and harsh summer sun, reaches 15 ft. (4.5 m) tall, male.

'**Blaauw**': vigorous with strongly ascending branches and short outer branches, dense gray-blue adult foliage, reaches 5 ft. (1.5 m) tall, nice for a small garden.

'**Blue Alps**': upright and vigorous spreading shrub with slightly pendulous prickly silvery blue-green foliage, red-brown bark, reaches 20 ft. (6 m) tall by 10 ft. (3 m) wide.

'**Daub's Frosted**': low-growing groundcover, two-toned foliage blue-green frosted with gold, quickly reaches 15 in. (38 cm) tall by 5 ft. (1.5 m) wide.

'**Gold Sovereign**': compact and slow-growing with bright yellow foliage year-round, reaches up to 20 ft. (6 m) tall with a wider spread.

Juniperus chinensis 'Aurea'

Juniperus chinensis 'Daub's Frosted'

Juniperus chinensis 'Gold Sovereign'

'Gold Star': compact with prickly golden yellow foliage in full sun, reaches 4 ft. (1.2 m) tall and a 6 ft. (1.8 m) spread.

'Kaizuka' (Hollywood juniper): irregular and upright with upward shoots that twist in various directions, dense moplike clusters of bright rich green scalelike foliage, violet-blue cones, makes an interesting accent or specimen plant, reaches 20 ft. (6 m) tall, can be trained against a wall, also known as 'Torulosa'.

'Obelisk': dense, narrow column, with prickly blue-green foliage, reaches 8 to 10 ft. (2.5 to 3 m) tall.

'Old Gold': compact to 3 ft. (0.9 m) high and a bit wider, yellow scalelike foliage in summer, becoming bronze in winter, sometimes listed under *Juniperus* ×*media*.

'Plumosa Aurea': flat-topped spreading form in arching sprays of adult foliage, golden yellow in summer, turning bronze in winter.

'Robust Green': broad, informal and craggy, ascending branches with blue-green prickly foliage in dense tufts, produces lots of cones, reaches 15 ft. (4.5 m) tall by 3 ft. (0.9 m) wide.

'San José': low-growing, irregularly spreading, very hardy, gray-green mixed foliage, 12 in.

Juniperus chinensis 'Gold Star'

Juniperus chinensis 'Old Gold'

Juniperus chinensis 'Plumosa Aurea' in late summer

Juniperus chinensis 'Plumosa Aurea' in late winter

(30 cm) tall, tough, widely grown, often suffers from phomopsis tip blight.

'Saybrook Gold': low and wide-spreading with center depression, horizontal branches arch slightly and droop at tips, persistent soft bright yellow juvenile foliage, doesn't always age well, 30 in. (75 cm) tall with a 6 ft. (1.8 m) spread, also listed as a selection of *Juniperus* ×*media* or *J.* ×*pfitzeriana*.

'Stricta': pyramidal habit, branches ascend to a point, prickly gray-blue foliage.

'Variegated Kaizuka': similar to 'Kaizuka' in habit but slower growing and with creamy yellow variegated foliage.

Juniperus communis
Common juniper
Zones 2 to 6

There is a reason this is called the common juniper. It is found across the Northern Hemisphere from North America through Europe and Asia to Japan and Korea. It is one of only three conifers native to Great Britain. Common juniper is found in every possible site, from high, dry, and alkaline to marshy and acid. Numerous "varieties" of this species are listed in the literature, many of which are yet to be sorted out by botanists.

Juniperus chinensis 'Variegated Kaizuka'

Juniperus chinensis 'Saybrook Gold'

JUNIPERUS COMMUNIS

This species sometimes is a small tree but more often is a large shrubby plant with a flat top. It typically has a rather slow growth rate. Its entirely juvenile awl-shaped needled (prickly) foliage is very stiff and in whorls of three with a blue-white strip on the upper surface. The needles always grow straight out from the stem, never embracing it as in some other species. The fleshy seed-bearing cones are twice the size of *Juniperus virginiana*.

There are around 105 cultivars. These garden selections like full sun and tolerate windy conditions. They also thrive in poor, rocky soils. Many dwarf forms exist with variations of foliage color. The species is not tolerant of heat.

The wood of the common juniper has been used to produce charcoal and to smoke meat. The "berries" are used to flavor game and gin.

'Berkshire': slow-growing little bun, prickly dark green foliage with striking silver white bands which give it a gray-green to blue-green appearance, bronzes in winter, to 1 ft. (0.3 m) tall.

'Compressa': slow-growing narrow upright dwarf, cone-shaped without shearing, fine-textured silvery blue-green foliage, grows 2 in. (5 cm) a year to 3 ft. (0.9 m) tall.

'Echiniformis' (hedgehog juniper): tiny, tight, prickly foliage in soft-appearing mounds, very slow-growing, syn. 'Hemispherica', sometimes listed under *Juniperus chinensis*.

'Gold Cone': slow-growing narrow and columnar shrub or small tree, dense foliage, golden in summer, yellow-green in winter, needs protection from sun and wind.

'Green Carpet': a slow-growing prostrate mat of bright green juvenile foliage, hardy and

Juniperus communis 'Compressa'

Juniperus communis 'Gold Cone'

Juniperus communis 'Green Carpet' grown as standard

Juniperus communis 'Haverbeck'

adaptable, ideal for slopes and rock or trough gardens.

'Haverbeck': dense blue-gray mixed foliage, reaches 1 ft. (0.3 m) tall in eight years.

'Hibernica' (Irish juniper): pillar-shaped with dense and compact vertical branches to 25 ft. (8 m) high, pale green needles with silver band on upper surface produces a blue-green effect, requires protection from wind and heavy snow.

'Hornibrookii': spreading and ground-hugging, prickly green needles are silver below, true plant is slow-growing and male but various forms are found in the trade.

'Horstmann': spreading and irregular with prickly pendulous blue-green foliage, grows up to 12 in. (30 cm) a year, accepts pruning.

'Pencil Point': pillar-shaped, tight light green foliage with silver bands giving a blue-green appearance, probably same as 'Sentinel'.

'Prostrata': ground-hugging form, reaches 1 ft. (0.3 m) tall by 4 to 6 ft. (1.2 to 1.8 m) wide.

Juniperus communis 'Hornibrookii'

Juniperus communis 'Pencil Point'

'**Repanda**': vigorous creeping form, sets new roots as it scrambles and forms a uniform circle, tips of branches nod, soft dark green foliage in summer, bronzy in winter, 15 in. (38 cm) high and 8 ft. (2.5 m) wide.

'**Sentinel**': upright and columnar, almost pointed without shearing, blue-green foliage, reaches 5 ft. (1.5 m) tall.

Juniperus conferta
Shore juniper
Zones 5 to 9

The shore juniper is native to the seasides of Japan. This slow-growing but generally vigorous species is most often used as a groundcover for sunny, well-drained or sandy seaside conditions. It tolerates poor soil but not moist soil. It is salt-tolerant. The foliage is needlelike, soft, but sharp-tipped and deeply grooved, with a white band above. It is usually a bushy, procumbent shrub that spreads across the ground with the tips of the advancing growth pointing upward.

Juniperus conferta 'Blue Lagoon' foliage

Juniperus conferta 'Blue Pacific'

The seed-bearing cones are spherical, about ½ in. (1.2 cm) round, silvery or blue-black, with a waxy bloom. Many of the cultivars are useful for container or rock gardens.

'**Blue Lagoon**': dense spreading mat with prickly foliage, green needles with blue overtones, single white band on each needle, turns plum in winter, 1 ft. (0.3 m) tall by 9 ft. (2.7 m) wide.

'**Blue Pacific**': spreading mat with prickly foliage, green with blue and silver overtones, does not bronze in winter, also listed as a selection of *Juniperus rigida* subsp. *conferta*.

'**Silver Mist**': salt-tolerant prostrate form with densely growing intensely silvery blue prickly foliage.

Juniperus horizontalis
Creeping juniper
Zones 4 to 9

The creeping juniper is native to North America from Newfoundland to Alaska, and south to Wyoming, Nebraska, northern Illinois, and northern New York. It is common in the Adirondacks in open, dry, sandy, and rocky habitats. Most selections of this species are prostrate. They are hardy enough to grow in areas as different as the seashore and mountain slopes. They typically have long main branches with many short, dense branchlets. The leaves on the cultivated forms are mainly needle-shaped,

Juniperus horizontalis 'Douglasii'

often in whorls of three, green or blue-green, and frequently turn mauve in the winter. The soft adult foliage can be found on older growth.

Many selections are slow-growing at first but become vigorous groundcovers useful for massing. They tolerate all types of soil but, typical of junipers, prefer full sun and good drainage. There are many more cultivars of this species in the catalogs than actually needed.

'Bar Harbor': dense mat of soft steel-blue scalelike foliage, turns a delicate mauve-purple in winter, branches spread and root in all directions with ascending tips, tolerates salt spray, does not produce cones.

'Blue Chip': a dense mounded carpet of soft and feathery bright silver blue-green foliage year-round, reaches 10 in. (25 cm) tall by 6 ft. (1.8 m) wide.

'Douglasii' (Waukegan juniper): wide-spreading and low-growing with mixed foliage, gray-green in summer, bronzed in cold weather, very small needles clasp the stem on semi-erect branchlets, useful in dune gardens.

Juniperus horizontalis Icee Blue ('Monber')

'Golden Carpet': prostrate with greenish yellow foliage.

'Green Acres': trailing and dense with dark green foliage year-round.

Icee Blue ('Monber'): the selling name says it all, reaches 4 in. (10 cm) tall by 8 ft. (2.5 m) wide.

'**Limeglow**': billowy foliage with brilliant chartreuse color even in hot summers.

'**Mother Lode**': brilliant gold in summer turning to shades of deep gold and salmon-orange with green overtones in winter, provide full sun with good drainage, very slow-growing, similar to 'Golden Carpet'.

'**Plumosa**' **(Andorra juniper)**: vigorous flat-topped spreading shrub, branches radiate from center of plant, dense prickly foliage gray-green

Juniperus horizontalis 'Limeglow'

Juniperus horizontalis 'Wiltonii'

Juniperus horizontalis 'Mother Lode'

in summer, bronze-purple in winter, to 20 in. (50 cm) high, widely grown, often suffers from phomopsis tip blight.

'**Prince of Wales**': low-growing and broad-spreading, dense, soft-appearing bright green foliage with a hint of blue, 4 to 6 in. (10 to 15 cm) high.

'**Wiltonii**': one of the best ground-hugging forms, slow growing with glaucous blue scale-like foliage on long branches, color maintained throughout the year, produces cones, 6 in. (15 cm) tall by 6 ft. (1.8 m) wide, also known as 'Blue Rug'.

'**Youngstown**': groundcover with tightly knit branches that turn up at a 45° angle, takes limited shade, bronzes in winter.

Juniperus ×*pfitzeriana* '*Gold Coast*'
Gold Coast Pfitzer juniper
Zones 4 to 9

This Pfitzer juniper selection is a semi-prostrate, flat-topped, wide-spreading shrub with bright yellow foliage. It is also fast growing and hardy, tolerating most any soil condition in heat and cold as long as it is provided good drainage. In the garden it is useful as a ground covering shrub.

'Gold Coast' is a confirmed member of the Pfitzer Group (*Juniperus* ×*pfitzeriana*), a cross between the Chinese juniper (*J. chinensis*) and the savin juniper (*J. sabina*). In the United States, Pfitzer junipers are often listed as cultivars of *J. chinensis*, while in Europe they are listed as cultivars of *J.* ×*media*.

Juniperus ×*pfitzeriana* 'Gold Coast'

Like other Pfitzer junipers, 'Gold Coast' has both prickly juvenile and soft adult scalelike foliage. The bright yellow adult foliage holds its color in winter.

Juniperus procumbens 'Nana'
Nana garden juniper
Zones 4 to 8(9)

Juniperus procumbens is a popular species in Japan, where it is native, but it is never found outside of that country. Instead, it is represented by the widely planted 'Nana', which slowly forms a compact mat less than 1 ft. (0.3 m) tall but spreading up to 8 ft. (2.5 m) wide. The layered branches vary in length, and the needlelike foliage is very prickly and remains distinctly blue-green in all seasons. This is an ideal conifer for placing at the top of a low stone wall or at the corner of steps to soften sharp corners. It is often used for bonsai.

Juniperus scopulorum
Rocky Mountain juniper
Zones 3 to 7

The Rocky Mountain juniper is native from British Columbia and Alberta south to Texas and is the most widespread juniper in western North America. It typically grows at elevations of 5000 ft. (1500 m) but can also be found near sea level. It is usually seen as a columnar tree up to 50 ft. (15 m) tall but is often a ragged little shrub on poor sites.

This hardy species prefers good drainage in sunny situations with dry air and is often seen on dry rocky ridges or sandy soils (the Latin *scopulus* means "cliff" or "rock"). It needs only 10 in. (25

Juniperus procumbens 'Nana'

Juniperus scopulorum 'Blue Arrow'

cm) of rainfall annually. It is slow-growing and can live hundreds of years.

The foliage is scalelike except in saplings, where it is awl-like. Some selections have an arresting silver-blue appearance. The foliage is pungent when crushed. The branches can be spreading, ascending and/or drooping. The bark is thin, red or gray, and shreds in long strips.

The wood is close-grained and very aromatic, like that of *Juniperus virginiana* (eastern red-cedar). Unlike other junipers, the Rocky Mountain juniper produces male and female cones on the same plant. Cones can persist for several years. There are over 100 cultivars.

'Blue Arrow': compact small tree with a narrow upright habit, 12 to 15 ft. (3.6 to 4.5 m) tall by 2 ft. (0.6 m) wide, blue-gray, similar to 'Skyrocket' but not quite as blue.

'Skyrocket': very narrow, 15 ft. (4.5 m) tall by 2 ft. (0.6 m) wide, blue-green, darkens in winter, use as a vertical accent or in a formal design, male, does not age well.

Juniperus squamata
Flaky juniper, singleseed juniper
Zones 4 to 7

This species is not usually found in designed landscapes. It is more important for the characteristics it has passed on to its cultivars, some of which are the most popular conifers used in gardens today.

Juniperus squamata is found in higher elevations in Afghanistan and east to central China.

Juniperus squamata 'Blue Carpet'

Quite variable in nature but usually shrub-sized, it is a drought-tolerant and resilient plant. The selections have needlelike foliage, and some a concentrated blue coloration. Flaky juniper usually displays nodding tips to the shoots. The cones are fleshy and glossy black and contain only a single seed. The reddish brown bark is scaly. There are a dozen or more cultivars.

'**Blue Carpet**': fast-growing horizontal sprays reach only 12 in. (30 cm) high but 6 ft. (1.8 m) wide, silver-blue foliage turning gray-green in winter, easy to grow.

'**Blue Star**': irregular slow-growing mound of dense blue foliage changing to a purplish heather-blue in winter, does best in full sun, grows to 16 in. (40 cm) high, is sometimes grafted on standards.

'**Holger**': dense and wide-spreading with sharply pointed pale yellow new foliage, turns gray-green in summer, reaches 3 ft. (0.9 m) tall by 4 ft. (1.2 m) wide.

'**Meyeri**': upright branches arch out every which way with drooping tips, up to 20 ft. (6 m) tall, dense, prickly silver-blue foliage, slightly off-color in winter, beautiful when well grown and given renewal pruning.

Juniperus virginiana
Eastern red-cedar
Zones 3 to 9

Eastern red-cedar is the most widespread native conifer in eastern North America. It is found from Nova Scotia to northern Florida and west to the Dakotas and Texas. Despite its common name, the tree is really a juniper and not a true cedar. It grows slowly to 20 to 50 ft. (6 to 15 m) in height. Younger trees are often narrow and columnar, but with age they become rounder and irregular. The species is found on hillsides and in abandoned fields, along roadsides, or in any dry, rocky situation. An undisturbed specimen can live 300 years.

The adult foliage is mostly scalelike, but younger plants have juvenile foliage as do the shadier and inner sections of mature specimens. On typical shoots, the scalelike blunt-tipped leaves are arranged opposite to each other in groups of four, closely appressed to the branchlet, dark bluish green, and persisting for a half-dozen years. The juvenile leaves are found on vigorous shoots and shady interior areas. They are $1/4$ to $1/2$ in. (0.6 to 1.2 cm) long, sharply pointed and awl-shaped. They are primarily in pairs.

Juniperus squamata 'Blue Star'

The pollen-bearing cones, 1/8 to 1/4 in. (0.3 to 0.6 cm) long and yellowish, appear terminally in early spring. The seed-bearing cones on different trees are 1/4 in. (0.6 cm) in diameter, fleshy like a berry with a firm, waxy skin and sweet-tasting flesh. They mature in two to three years and contain one or two seeds. They smell like gin when crushed. The cones are pale green at first and mature to a dark blue and are covered with a whitish bloom. Trees begin producing cones at 10 to 15 years of age. The bark is light reddish brown and exfoliates in long narrow strips. The trunk is often buttressed and fluted at the base.

This species is not finicky about soil quality but grows best in full sun with good drainage. This tough tree tolerates drought, heat, and cold and difficult site situations where other conifers struggle. It is especially valuable for gardeners in the Midwest and Plains states. Among the many cultivars are some that provide abundant blue seed-bearing cones. The species tends to bronze in the winter, so selection has been made for cultivars that stay green all year. Both upright and semi-prostrate forms can be had.

The wood is extremely durable in contact with the soil and has traditionally been used for fence posts and outdoor structures. The pungent deep red heartwood is easy to work with and is used for making moth-proof chests for garment storage, interior paneling for spas, and pencils. Cedar oil, a component of popular furniture polishes, is extracted from the foliage and wood. Many birds feast on the berrylike cones during the winter, notably the cedar waxwing, which is named after this "cedar." The seed is dispersed by the birds everywhere.

As an ornamental plant, *Juniperus virginiana* is especially useful for very dry, full-sun locations. It is a tough plant and has 85 cultivars.

Cedar-apple rust (*Gymnosporangium juniperi-virginianae*) is a fungal disease that spends part of its life cycle on the eastern red-cedar and another part on apple or hawthorn trees. Both hosts are necessary for the survival of the fungus and can be up to 5 miles (8.3 km) apart. The disease can cause defoliation of the apple and hawthorn species in periods of drought. Galls as large as golf balls are formed on the juniper host during the second year of the complicated cycle, causing small twig and

Juniperus virginiana adult foliage and seed-bearing cones

tip dieback. One should select species, particularly crabapples, that are resistant to rust diseases. Resistant *Juniperus virginiana* cultivars include 'Burkii' and 'Kosteri'. *Juniperus virginiana* can also be troubled with scale (see the discussion at *Thuja*).

'Blue Arrow': narrow and upright, retains lower branches, foliage deep blue.

'Burkii': columnar with a straight stem and ascending branches, dense blue-green mixed foliage, bronzes in winter.

Juniperus virginiana 'Burkii' in winter

'Canaertii': upright, eventually opens up, dense dark green foliage year-round, tufted at the ends of the branches, abundant blue cones.

'Corcorcor': narrow and conical, remains a rich green in all seasons, rapid growing, sturdy and dependable, reaches 25 to 30 ft. (8 to 9 m) tall, also called 'Emerald Sentinel'.

'Grey Owl': soft dusty silver-gray foliage and abundant silver-gray cones, grows slowly into a wide-spreading shrub 3 ft. (0.9 m) tall by 6 ft. (1.8 m) wide. Exceptional.

'Hillspire': upright conical habit, bright green foliage year-round on densely packed branches, male, can reach 30 ft. (9 m) tall.

'Kosteri': compact 4 ft. (1.2 m) tall but can spread to 30 ft. (9 m) wide in time, gray-blue foliage bronzes in winter.

Juniperus virginiana 'Canaertii' foliage and cones

Juniperus virginiana 'Grey Owl'

LARIX
Larch

Larix, along with *Ginkgo*, *Metasequoia* (dawn redwood), *Pseudolarix* (golden-larch), and *Taxodium* (bald-cypress), comprises deciduous plants that drop their foliage each winter. The approximately ten species of larches are widely distributed across North America, Asia, and Europe, and can be found growing from lowland habitats to subalpine conditions.

Although the various species have many similarities in appearance to the casual observer, they differ in their cultural requirements and plant communities as well as in the details of their cones and needles. Still, some authorities disagree about the divisions of *Larix* species and subspecies.

A number of *Larix* cultivars are suitable for the designed landscape. The great attraction of larches to the gardener is their light green foliage in the growing season, their golden flash of fall color, and, in some cases, their austere winter habit.

Description

Most larches are rather fast-growing to heights of 100 ft. (30 m) and are too large for the average garden. The trees usually develop a single central trunk. Their branches are often pendulous with clusters of needles held on short shoots called spurs. Each of these clusters holds many needles of differing lengths. New shoots have needles spiraling singly around the stem. The needles are generally an appealing lime-green in early spring and turn a luminous gold in autumn. The small pollen-bearing cones are yellow and often appear on bare stems. The seed-bearing cones appear in early spring and are vibrantly colored; they ripen in one year and are held upright on the stem. The dark-colored mature cones often persist on the tree for years.

ID Features

The genus *Larix* is easy to recognize, but the various species are difficult to sort out. The cones of *L. laricina* (American larch) are the smallest; those of *L. decidua* (European larch) and *L. kaempferi* (Japanese larch) are two to three times larger, but the cone scales of the Japanese larch are reflexed. Although the foliage of *Larix* species looks a bit like that of *Cedrus* (cedar), the needles of *Cedrus* are unkind to the touch and those of *Larix* are soft. Of course, the cones are completely different.

Cultivation

Full sun is recommended for all species.

Pests and Diseases

The European larch casebearer (*Coleophora laricella*) infects all larches in the United States. This insect eats the inside tissue of needles and causes defoliation. It lives in a case made from sections of hollowed-out needles during part of its life cycle. Casebearers cause the most damage to larches in spring when they feed on the new foliage. Since larches are deciduous, they can tolerate repeated defoliations but eventually branch tips and entire branches will die. The pest is weakened by late frosts and is eaten by various insects, spiders, and birds. Several insect parasites have been introduced to reduce casebearer populations.

Uses

Most larches are more important in forestry than as ornamental plants. Several are valued for their wood, which is strong, heavy, and durable.

Larix decidua
European larch
Zones 3 to 6(7)

This larch is native to Europe east to Siberia and is the only deciduous conifer native in Europe. Rapidly growing and very hardy, the tree is much planted in eastern North America for timber and occasionally as a specimen.

The European larch has a conical habit up to 75 ft. (23 m) tall with branches held horizontally but drooping at the tips. The twigs display short shoots that are brown-black with rings from each year's growth. The ½ to 1½ in. (1.2 to 3.5 cm) long needles are held in whorls of 30 to 40 on

Larix decidua seed-bearing cones and foliage

Larix decidua fall foliage

short spurs but held singly on tip growth. The needles are of unequal length, bright green when young, deeper green in summer, and turning mustard-yellow in autumn. The pollen-bearing cones are rounded and yellow, appearing in spring. The seed-bearing cones are 1 to 1½ in. (2.5 to 3.5 cm) long with numerous scales that are rounded and not reflexed. They are stalkless with pubescent scales, mature reddish brown, and persist on the tree. The bark is red-brown and platy.

Larix decidua is adapted to much drier habitats than other larches. It tolerates poor soil but not pollution. In the wild it is often found in wet areas. It demands full sun. One would grow this as a specimen in a large landscape to admire its beautiful pristine pale green spring foliage and lustrous gold fall display. It is an important tree for reforestation. The durable wood is used for posts, shipbuilding, and general construction.

'**Horstmann Recurved**': twisted and contorted branches on an irregularly shaped tree, bright green in spring turning gold in autumn, reaches 7 ft. (2 m) tall in ten years.

'**Pendula**': fast growing, variable from widespreading to narrow, needs staking or could be used as a groundcover. Many specimens in the trade with this label are actually *Larix kaempferi* 'Pendula'.

'**Puli**': weeping form used as groundcover or cascading from the highest point of staking, vivid golden yellow fall color.

'**Varied Directions**': wider than tall, branches go out and up from this vigorous spreading

Larix decidua 'Horstmann Recurved' foliage

Larix decidua bark

Larix decidua 'Puli'

Larix decidua 'Varied Directions'

plant, then arch down and cover the ground, sometimes grafted as a high standard, also listed as *Larix* ×*eurolepsis*, *L. sibirica*, or a hybrid between *L. decidua* and *L. kaempferi*.

Larix kaempferi
Japanese larch
Zones 4 to 7

The Japanese larch is native to Honshu. It is similar to *Larix decidua* except the needles have two distinct longitudinal bands on the bottom, young branches are glaucous, and the cones have reflexed cone scales.

This strong-growing, large tree becomes 70 to 90 ft. (21 to 27 m) tall and 25 to 40 ft. (8 to 12 m) wide with a straight trunk. It can be narrow and conical or wide-spreading with long horizontal branches and slender pendulous branchlets. The pale green 1/2 to 1 3/4 in. (1.2 to 4.5 cm) long needles are in tufts of 40 to 50. The pollen-bearing cones are dark red-brown in clusters. The seed-bearing cones are egg-shaped on short stalks and 3/4 to 1 1/4 in. (2 to 3 cm) long. The upper edges of the cone scales are rolled back, giving a rosettelike appearance. The fall foliage color is golden (not just yellow). The tree has reddish exfoliating bark, and the twigs appear reddish in the winter landscape. These twigs help differentiate the Japanese larch from the European larch. The Japanese larch also has more widely spaced branches on a more massive trunk, giving it a more open form.

This is a tree for large, sunny landscapes. It is adaptable to lowland and wet areas, tolerates clay soils, and is disease-resistant.

'Blue Rabbit': narrow and conical with blue foliage, reaches 70 ft. (21 m) tall and 15 ft. (4.5 m) wide, is often grown on a standard as 'Blue Rabbit Weeping'.

'Diana': a small upright tree with graceful branching, curled and twisted branches, needles are also twisted, can be pruned to desired size or grown in a tub, reaches 12 ft. (3.6 m) tall by 8 ft. (2.5 m) wide in ten years, also listed as 'Diane'.

'Pendula': weeping habit or prostrate unless grafted onto a stake and permitted to drape to the ground, often sold as *Larix decidua* 'Pendula' or *L. decidua* 'Julian's Weeping'.

'Stiff Weeping': similar to 'Pendula' except foliage is compact and close to trunk.

'Wolterdingen': dwarf, slow-growing, irregular conical growth reaches 20 in. (50 cm) tall by 24 in. (60 cm) wide in ten years, blue-green foliage.

Larix kaempferi foliage

Larix kaempferi 'Pendula'

Larix laricina 'Blue Sparkler'

Larix laricina
American larch, tamarack
Zones (1)2 to 5

This species is the most extensive of the three larch species found in North America and grows further north than any other tree on the continent. It is native from eastern Canada (it is a major species in Labrador) to the Yukon River and south into the northern central United States and eastward into Ohio, Pennsylvania, New Jersey, and New York. It grows to the high timberline, but in more southern locations it is usually found growing in areas where its roots are constantly wet. It is one of the widest-ranging conifers on the continent.

The American larch seldom forms pure stands but tends to grow where few other trees will survive. It rarely grows over 60 ft. (18 m) in height. The crown is narrowly conical and open, with horizontal branches and drooping branchlets. The root system is shallow. The trunk is straight, but the tree often becomes asymmetrical at maturity. Even a grove of these trees does not produce heavy shade. *Larix laricina* lives 150 years.

The pale green, soft and flexible, $1/2$ to $1 1/4$ in. (1.2 to 3 cm) needles emerge early in the spring. They are in clusters of 10 to 30 on short spurlike shoots, or solitary and spiraling around the stem on new shoots. The leaves turn golden yellow in fall and are shed. The pollen-bearing cones are bright yellow and round, hanging onto the twig. The seed-bearing cones are oblong with scarlet-colored scales that have long green tips. The mature chestnut-brown cones are $1/2$ to $3/4$ in. (1.2 to 2 cm) long on short stalks. They open in late summer to release their seeds. The cones are held erect on the stem and persist for several seasons. This larch begins bearing cones at age 12 to 15 and produces a good crop every three to six years. The bark is thin, scaly, and bright reddish brown.

This fast-growing, shallow-rooted species tolerates a wide range of (low) temperatures, rainfall, and amounts of daylight. It does not like heat; however, it should be given full sun. *Larix laricina* is not usually considered an attractive ornamental; the winter habit is somewhat cheerless. It not only survives in conditions that are far too wet for most woody plants but also grows well in them. It is seldom planted in England.

The wood is heavy, very strong, close-grained, and durable. Its traditional use was for railroad ties and utility poles. Native Americans used the roots for stitching together their birch-bark canoes. Even today boat builders bend and steam larch for frames of wooden boats. The resinous wood is susceptible to forest fires.

The American larch is not a plant one would choose for the benefit of wildlife, although porcupines love to climb these trees and eat the inner bark, which sometimes kills the tree. Grouse eat the needles and buds, and crossbills harvest the seeds.

'Blue Sparkler': vigorous grower with excellent blue foliage, reaches 5 ft. (1.5 m) tall at maturity, sometimes listed as a selection of *Larix kaempferi*.

'Craftsbury Flats': dwarf round ball of pale green foliage, matures at 4 ft. (1.2 m) tall.

Larix laricina 'Craftsbury Flats'

Metasequoia glyptostroboides fall color

Metasequoia glyptostroboides
Dawn redwood
Zones 4 to 8

This deciduous conifer was thought to be extinct until 1941, when a few trees were found in central China. Seeds were collected and distributed by the Arnold Arboretum in 1948 to many arboreta and public gardens, and the species is now widely planted in North America and Europe and available at most nurseries.

Dawn redwood is a vigorous, strong-growing tree. It can reach 100 ft. (30 m) in its native habitat, a small area in the provinces of Hubei and Sichuan. Under cultivation it reaches 40 to 50 ft. (12 to 15 m) tall in fewer than 20 years. It grows quickly, often 3 to 4 ft. (0.9 to 1.2 m) a year early on. It becomes broad and conical, very orderly and uniform, with a sharply pointed top on a central single stem (see photo on page 15). It has a very distinctive winter habit (see photo on page 22).

The ferny leaves are deciduous, two-ranked, and in an opposite arrangement. They are about ¾ in. (2 cm) long on the deciduous shoots. The leaves are bright green when they first emerge and become a shade darker during the growing season. The autumn color changes from a yellow-brown to pink, even apricot, then a copper-brown. The leaves fall attached to the twiglet. The pollen-bearing cones are in the axils of the deciduous shoots and open in early spring; they are borne in dangling racemes or panicles. The solitary seed-bearing cones are ¾ to 1 in. (2 to 2.5 cm) round on the ends of short side twigs. They ripen from green to brown in the first year. The orange to russet-brown bark becomes fissured with age and peels in long strips. The trunk becomes buttressed and irregularly fluted. Children call this the "armpit tree."

Dawn redwood tolerates very wet, even boggy soil for part of the year. It grows best in moist, deep soil but will grow on dry sites once established. It accepts pollution and urban conditions. It is more cold-hardy than the evergreen redwoods. Give it room and pull up a chair and watch it grow. It is an excellent tree to grow in groves where space is available.

Although the foliage looks similar, the way to tell the difference between this and another deciduous conifer, *Taxodium distichum* (bald-cypress), is that the latter has alternately arranged foliage and a completely different bark and trunk.

'Ogon': slower growing with bright gold-yellow foliage, needs some protection from scorching summer sun, also known as 'Gold Rush'. See additional photo on page 2.

'Sheridan Spire': narrow compact form with ascending limbs, bright green foliage, handsome orange-brown fall color, reaches 60 ft. (18 m) tall by 20 ft. (6 m) wide.

Metasequoia glyptostroboides buttressed trunk

Metasequoia glyptostroboides 'Ogon' foliage

Microbiota decussata on a slope

Microbiota decussata
Siberian cypress
Zones 2 to 8

The Siberian cypress is native to eastern Siberia, where it is found above the tree line in the mountains. The only species in the genus, it is a very cold hardy, dense, prostrate, juniper-like plant. It prefers cool conditions and demands good drainage but tolerates a wide range of soils. Unusually for a conifer, it prefers to grow in high shade, although it does well in full sun with adequate moisture.

Microbiota decussata is only about 12 in. (30 cm) high but is very wide-spreading, to 6 to 12 ft. (1.8 to 3.6 m). The soft, fine-textured, lacy leaves are in flat sprays that arch over with drooping tips. The foliage is pale green in summer and bronze to purple in winter. The species is reported to be dioecious, but most plants in cultivation are male clones and have inconspicuous cones. The slender stems are reddish brown.

This species is probably not a suitable choice for southern gardens. Under the right growing conditions (again, that means good drainage and cool), it forms a wide-spreading carpet and is excellent as a foundation plant or on slopes. It accepts open wind-exposed sites and combines well with upright plants. The Siberian cypress is worthy of much wider use.

PICEA
Spruce

Picea includes about 50 species, of which 7 are native to North America. They have a pyramidal form but often lose lower branches and become less attractive as they age. These rugged and adaptable trees are widely planted in the northern half of the United States, in England, and across Europe. In their native habitat many spruces are tall and narrow, but in cultivation they are often shorter and broader at the base

Description
The leaves are evergreen and needlelike, and can be all shades of green. The much-loved blue spruces have bluish needles. The needles are borne separately, not in bundles, and often crowd densely on the twig and spiral around in all directions. They are quadrangular in cross section and have a prickly barbed tip. The needles are attached to the twig by a small brown peg and remain on the tree for seven to ten years.

Spruces are monoecious. The pollen-bearing cones are cylindrical, fleshy, and held erect usually in the middle and lower part of the crown. The seed-bearing cones are in the upper part of the crown and become pendulous as they mature; they remain on the tree until the next growing season when they fall intact from the tree. Spruces often begin to form cones by the tenth year of growth.

ID Features
One way to distinguish *Picea* from *Abies* (fir) is to carefully remove a needle from its twig. If a piece of the twig epidermis pulls off with the needle, the plant is a spruce; if the needle comes off cleanly, the plant is a fir.

Another distinctive ID feature is that the twig of *Picea* is bumpy after the needles drop naturally because the small brown pegs which attach the needles to the stem remain on the stem.

A third distinction is that the mature seed-bearing cones of *Picea* hang down and drop intact, while the mature cones of *Abies* are held upright on the branch and disintegrate on the tree.

Cultivation
Spruces thrive in full sun and good drainage. Most of them prefer cooler, moister climates and often do not succeed in hot, dry conditions. They do not tolerate alkaline soils, salt spray, or urban pollution. Spruces need very little pruning. Their roots are shallow and fibrous. Plants do not perform as well when grown in a container and are best transplanted balled-and-burlapped in the spring.

Pests and Diseases
Adelgids (*Adelges* species) are aphidlike insects that produce disfiguring galls, which can be re-

Spruce cones hang down, the needles are held singly

Spruce twigs are bumpy

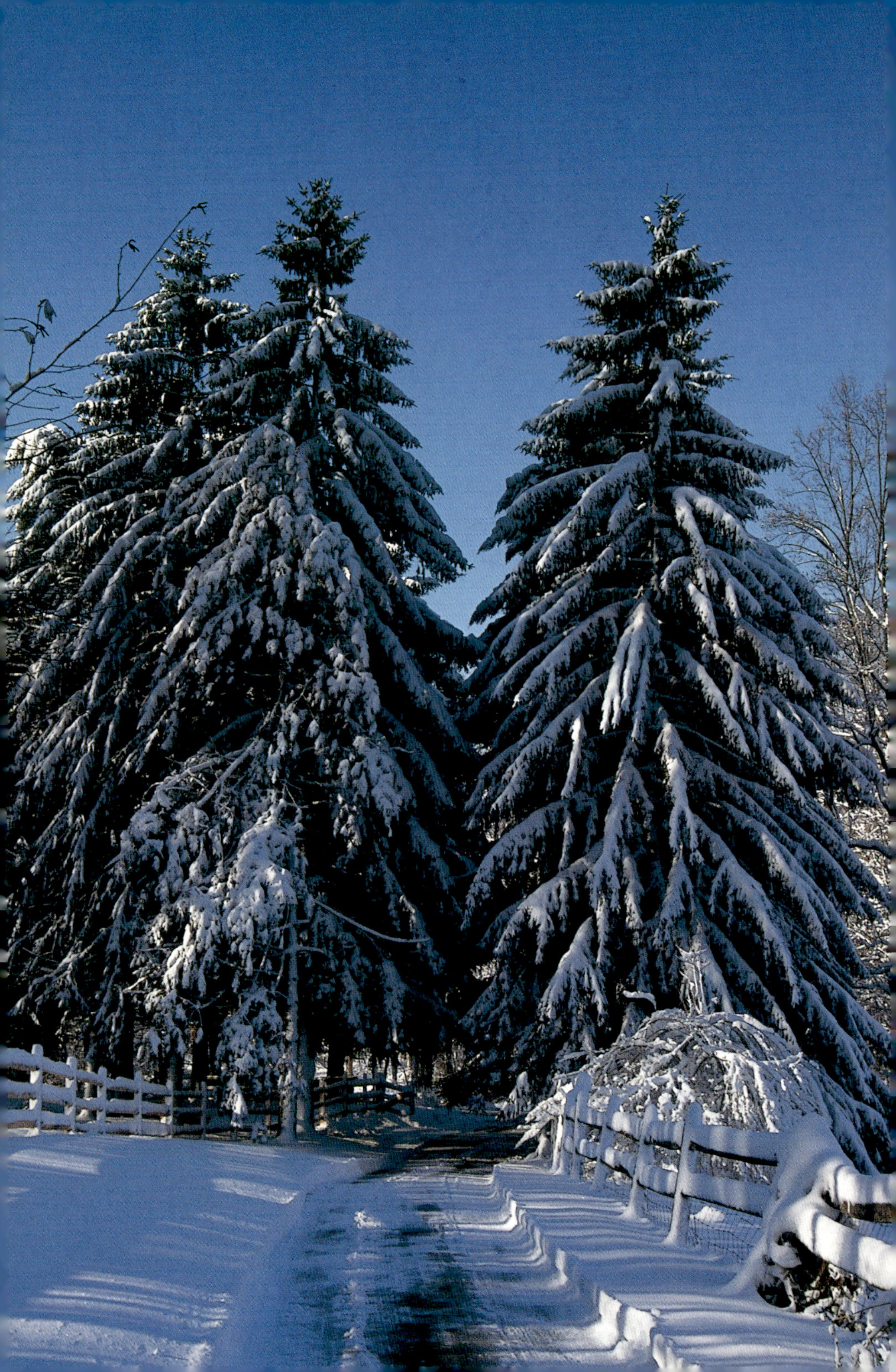

moved by hand or the affected branches pruned. Dormant-oil treatments can be applied spring or fall. Some adelgids overwinter on *Pseudotsuga menziesii* (Douglas-fir); any trees nearby also have to be treated.

Cytospora canker is caused by a fungal organism, *Cytospora kunzei*. The disease makes the needles turn brown and drop, and the branches turn brittle, starting at the bottom of the tree. The dead tissue on the bark is covered with a noticeable white resin. The fungal spores are spread by splashing rain, insects, and gardening tools. The disease is prevented by growing spruces under favorable conditions and avoiding mechanical injury to the bark and roots. Chemical control is not effective.

Another fungus that leads to a needle cast disorder is caused by *Rhizosphaera kalkhoffii*. Again, the needles turn brown and drop, starting with the lower branches.

Uses

Spruces are a major source of wood for construction. The wood is light, strong, and easy to work with. It has long fibers and a low resin content that make it ideal for pulp and paper products. The wood also is highly resonant and thus prized for the manufacturing of organ pipes, piano sounding boards, violins, guitars, and other stringed instruments.

Native Americans used the roots as thread for birch-bark canoes, baskets, and snowshoes. They also used the wood, gum, and foliage for a range of useful items.

The wildlife value of spruce is confined to northern animals. Grouses, especially the spruce grouse, Franklin grouse, and blue grouse, obtain much of their food from spruce needles. Rabbits and deer browse the foliage and twigs. Porcupines eat the bark. The small, winged seeds of spruce are a valuable food of the white-winged crossbill and several other kinds of birds, and are eaten by squirrels and chipmunks as well.

Opposite: Spruces bear snow well

Picea abies
Norway spruce
Zones 3 to 7

This conifer is native to central and northern Europe, where it is the most common *Picea* species and a very important timber tree. It has become the most widely used horticultural spruce in North America and the major introduced spruce used in reforestation in eastern Canada and northeastern United States.

The Norway spruce is huge, up to 100 ft. (30 m) tall and 40 ft. (12 m) wide. In Europe it can reach 200 ft. (60 m) tall. It develops into a wide pyramidal tree; the primary branches are upturned, but the secondary side branchlets usually become pendulous with age. This spruce is popular in large part because it grows fast, up to 2 ft. (0.6 m) a year. That it is widely available adds to its popularity as an ornamental. Unfortunately, gardeners often forget that it gets really big.

The dark green foliage often appears shiny, 1/2 to 1 in. (1.2 to 2.5 cm) long, pointing forward on the twigs. The stems are very rough after needle drop. The pollen-bearing cones are reddish, 1/2 to 3/4 in. (1.2 to 2 cm) long. The mature seed-bearing cones are cylindrical up to 9 in. (23 cm) long, light brown becoming reddish brown. They are pendulous and mature the first autumn but persist throughout the first winter. The cone scales are thin and round. The bark on older trunks becomes roughened with thick, flaky, reddish brown scales.

The tree prefers full sun but is very adaptable to a wide variety of soil conditions. It tolerates dry sites and wind. Often used as windbreak or screen, it can be sheared in the spring into a hedge. It tends to be healthier in cooler climates. It is easily transplanted. This spruce can be ugly when old, as the lower branches are shaded out and die. Like all the spruces, it tolerates snow well.

In the cultivated landscape the Norway spruce is widely employed (some would say overplanted) for its fast growth, tolerance, and foliage color. The dark green needles of this large tree make a wonderful backdrop for smaller trees with

Picea abies

interesting bark, flowers, or fall color. *Picea abies* is best known in Britain as a choice holiday tree. The light strong wood is widely used for lumber and pulp.

This species has an enormous natural variation. It also has more than 160 cultivars, which include many dwarfs effective for the home garden. It is often difficult to tell what distinguishes one cultivar from another.

'Acrocona': an irregular bush that eventually forms a leader, produces long red cones at the tips of its shoots even as a young plant, slow-growing and broad-spreading to 15 ft. (4.5 m) tall and wide.

'Cincinnata': a small "snake branch" tree (see 'Virgata') with pendulous branches.

'Clanbrassiliana': a dense flat-topped bush, wider than tall, only 3 ft. (0.9 m) tall after decades. Choice.

'Cranstonii': an irregularly growing bush with an open habit and long loose branches, spare and snakelike, reaches 40 ft. (12 m) tall by 20 ft. (6 m) wide, this and 'Virgata' for those who like freaky conifers.

'Echiniformis': a slow-growing compact shrub with prickly congested foliage above a wide-spreading skirt, 5 ft. (1.5 m) tall by 11 ft. (3.4 m) wide after decades.

Picea abies 'Acrocona' cones in spring

Picea abies 'Echiniformis'

Picea abies 'Elegantissima'

'Elegantissima': a pendulous form, growing 1 ft. (0.3 m) a year with gold-yellow foliage early in season, turning green by autumn.

'Formanek': a prostrate, eventually dense-spreading mat, useful in rock gardens.

'Frohburg': a slow-growing, prostrate shrub with weeping branches, can be trained into sculptural forms, has short medium green needles, often narrow, strict weeping habit with a full spreading skirt.

'Gold Drift': a weeping form with yellow foliage that burns in full sun, can be staked to desired height.

'Gregoryana': a dwarf, tight flat-topped bun 18 in. (46 cm) tall and wide, reaching 4 ft. (1.2 m) tall after many years.

Picea abies 'Gold Drift'

'**Inversa**': a vigorous weeping tree, needs to be trained on a stake to the desired height and then allowed to drape, frequently has unusual shapes, if not staked will be 20 ft. (6 m) wide and only 4 ft. (1.2 m) tall, often called 'Pendula'.

'**Little Gem**': a tight flat dome of dense branches with small light green soft needles, grows 1 to 2 in. (2.5 to 5 cm) a year. See photo on page 133.

'**Maxwellii**': a very slow-growing tight bun similar to 'Gregoryana' but larger with sharp light green needles, maturing into a flat-topped mound.

'**Mucronata**': a broadly pyramidal form with dense bright blue-green foliage, irregular when young, 15 to 30 ft. (4.5 to 9 m) tall.

'**Nidiformis**' (**bird's nest spruce**): a dwarf shrub reaching 3 ft. (0.9 m) high and 5 ft. (1.5 m) wide in 10 to 15 years with a depression in the center of its flat top, widely available and planted in gardens as a foundation plant.

'**Pendula**': a weeping habit that tends to stay low unless trained upright on a post, may

Picea abies 'Inversa' underplanted with *Nepeta racemosa* 'Walker's Low'

Picea abies 'Nidiformis'

Picea abies 'Pendula', low growing form

Picea abies 'Pendula' trained upright

be the same as 'Inversa' in the trade, dark green needles, some specimens grow in all directions with a carpet at the base. A collective name and sometimes listed as f. *pendula*.

'Perry's Gold': a small cone-shaped plant, growing only 4 in. (10 cm) a year, bright yellow in spring, turning green in summer, said to have best color in part shade.

Picea abies 'Perry's Gold'

Picea abies 'Procumbens'

Picea abies 'Pumila'

'Procumbens': a wide-spreading plant with stiff sprays of foliage and a flat top, slow-growing, similar to 'Repens'.

'Prostrata': ground-hugging and wide-spreading, mounds a bit with age, light green in summer, darker with cool weather.

'Pumila': slow-growing, dense flat-topped and spreading, sometimes irregular, dark green shiny foliage, similar to 'Nidiformis' and 'Repens' but better for cold climates because it breaks bud later in the spring.

'Pygmaea': an extremely slow-growing, compact shrub becoming broad and dome-shaped, reaches 18 in. (46 cm) tall after many years. Outstanding selection.

'Reflexa': similar to 'Inversa' but coarser, with larger needles.

'Repens': slow-growing, flat-topped, center builds up in time, dark green foliage, shorter and more spreading than 'Nidiformis'.

'Saint James': very small, bun-shaped with olive-green leaves, red buds in spring.

'Virgata' (snake branch spruce): long, whorled, sparsely produced thick branches with few secondary branchlets, grows 3 ft. (0.9 m) a year, sometimes listed as f. *virgata*.

Picea abies 'Repens'

Picea abies 'Virgata'

Picea abies 'Wingle's Weeper'

'Wingle's Weeper': a weeping habit with an upright spiraling leader, developing a full skirt in time, growing 10 in. (25 cm) a year.

Picea glauca
White spruce
Zones 2 to 6

The white spruce is the most widespread native conifer in North America. It is found throughout Canada and the northern United States, where the vast forests of this tree look almost black. The tree grows on the banks of streams and lakes and other wet areas as well as on ocean cliffs. It can reach 150 ft. (46 m) tall in the Canadian Rockies but is usually half that size in cultivation. It can live 200 years. Conical in outline with dense foliage and downward-sweeping boughs, the tree keeps its branches to the ground in open areas.

The blue-green or pale green needles are crowded and twisted on the upper side of the twig, each ¼ in. to ¾ in. (0.6 to 2 cm) long, with a sharp tip. They tend to curl and look combed. The needles emit a pungent odor when crushed, leading to the common name of skunk spruce. The needles persist on the tree for seven to ten years. The cones are 2 in. (5 cm) long. They turn pale brown and are somewhat shiny. The mature bark is gray, tinged with brown, with thin scales and a cinnamon-brown inner bark.

This rather variable species is seldom placed in gardens, but a number of notable and hardy cultivars are available. It could be a useful large-scale spruce for cold climates.

In Canada the white spruce is valued as an important source of timber and pulpwood. The wood is light, straight-grained, and resilient and used for general construction. The pliable roots were used by First Nations peoples to lace birch-bark canoes. *Picea glauca* is the state tree of South Dakota and the provincial tree of Manitoba.

'Alberta Globe': a slow-growing, neat and rounded shrub with dense ¼ in. (0.6 cm) long needles, reaches 24 in. (60 cm) tall by 20 in. (50 cm) wide in ten years.

'Blue Planet': a dense flat globe.

Picea glauca dwarf collection

Picea glauca 'Blue Planet'

Picea glauca 'Conica' (center) in a border

Picea glauca 'Echiniformis'

'Cecilia': a compact form with short glossy dense silver-blue needles, slow-growing, flat and spreading.

'Conica' (dwarf Alberta spruce): a dense, conical shrub with light green foliage, widely available and planted but too often poorly grown. Becomes 3 to 4 ft. (0.9 to 1.2 m) tall by 18 in. (46 cm) wide in 10 to 15 years. Does best in a cool location with some shade and good air circulation; needs protection from hot and cold winds, reflected sunlight, and heat from walls. With maturity it is a glorious plant and wonderful accent in a mixed border, often used as a container plant. By nature it has a very neat conical and compact shape, looking like it has been devotedly trained. It never seems to lose this shape.

Picea glauca 'Jean's Dilly' with *P. abies* 'Little Gem' as groundcover

It is a retreat for spider mites because of its tight foliage. Deer do not usually browse on it. It is often labeled 'Albertiana Conica'. Many of the other cultivars in this listing are simply bud sports of 'Conica'. Zones 3 to 7.

'Daisy's White': flushes white new foliage in spring, grows 2 in. (5 cm) a year.

'Echiniformis': has a low pillow shape with short, thin, gray-green needles, good for trough gardens because of its extremely slow growth, becomes bluer with age.

'Gnome': a very slow-growing columnar form.

'Jean's Dilly': slower growing than 'Conica', even more tailored and darker green.

Picea glauca 'Pixie'

'Laurin': a slow-growing cone, reaches only 10 in. (25 cm) tall.

'Little Globe': has a rounded dense habit, grows only 1 in. (2.5 cm) a year, good for rock gardens.

'Pixie': a slow-growing, upright narrow cone with dark green needles, reaches 12 in. (30 cm) tall in ten years.

Picea glauca 'Pixie Dust'

Picea glauca 'Rainbow's End'

'Pixie Dust': dense and compact, emerging bud growth is yellow, reaches 16 in. (40 cm) tall in ten years.

'Rainbow's End': similar to 'Conica' but has creamy yellow new growth, benefits from light shade to avoid burning.

'Sander's Blue': has tight conical growth, soft slate-blue foliage but unfortunate tendency to revert to green.

'Zuckerhut': a dwarf with green foliage.

Picea omorika
Serbian spruce
Zones 4 to 7

The Serbian spruce is native to Bosnia and Serbia. Although it has a very limited natural range, it is very adaptable and has broad ornamental potential. It generally forms one trunk and reaches a height of 60 ft. (18 m). The tall, very stylish tree is slender with short drooping branches that curve upward at the tips. Since this species tends to remain rather narrow, it is great for suburban gardens.

The ½ to 1 in. (1.2 to 2.5 cm) needles are rather flat, glossy dark green on one side and

Picea glauca 'Sander's Blue'

glaucous on the other. The whitish undersides of the flat needles make the tree look flushed with silver. It is a very graceful two-toned spruce. The pollen-bearing cones are light red. The violet, 1 ½ to 2½ in. (3.5 to 6 cm) seed-bearing cones appear in clusters.

This spruce should be planted in full sun on well-drained soil. It tolerates heat, humidity, and wind, and is not damaged by snow. Many consider it a good choice for urban landscapes because it tolerates air pollution better than most spruces and is also forbearing of limestone soil. It is resistant to the pests and diseases that plague many other spruces.

The Serbian spruces are usually seedling grown, but some are grafted on *Picea abies* (Norway spruce) rootstock. The plants are easy to transplant but should not be allowed to dry out until established. They usually grow 12 to 18 in. (30 to 46 cm) a year. Plants from lower elevations seem to achieve larger sizes and are wider than those originating from higher habitats.

Picea omorika has always been widely planted in Germany. It is magnificent either as a specimen or in a grouping. It is very flammable and it is non-allergenic.

'Aurea': habit like the species but with yellow foliage.

'Nana': a broadly conical shrub with two-toned needles, eventually becomes pyramidal, reaches 3 ft. (0.9 m) tall in ten years, ideal for small gardens.

'Pendula': has an upright central leader with very vertical pendulous branches and a trailing skirt, slower growing than the species.

Picea omorika upturned branch tips

Picea omorika 'Nana'

Picea omorika 'Pendula' with *Juniperus horizontalis* 'Mother Lode' as groundcover

Picea omorika 'Pendula Bruns'

'**Pendula Bruns**': a very narrow selection with strongly pendulous side branches. Stunning.

'**Pimoko**': a broad-growing bun, short blue-green needles with silver undersides on short branches, smaller than 'Nana', good for rock gardens.

'**Treblitzsch**': a compact cushion with coarse foliage.

Picea orientalis
Oriental spruce
Zones 4 to 7

The oriental spruce is native to southeastern Europe and southwestern Asia. It is a beautifully shaped pyramidal tree reaching 60 ft. (18 m) tall by 20 ft. (6 m) wide, densely branched with graceful, very dark green foliage that is maintained to the ground. It does not tend to get as wide as *Picea abies* (Norway spruce) and does not grow quite as fast, 8 to 12 in. (20 to 30 cm) a year.

The soft, glossy, dark green needles are shorter than those of any other spruce, only $1/4$ to $1/2$ in. (0.6 to 1.2 cm) long, thick, and close to the twig. They stay on the branch for up to four years. The new growth is regularly a lighter green. The pollen-bearing cones are often bright red before shedding pollen. The pendulous seed-bearing cones are 2 to 4 in. (5 to 10 cm) long, purple when young, turning brown with age. The bark is brown with some exfoliation.

Picea orientalis does best in full sun but tolerates light shade. It is relatively tolerant of drought and wind, but gardeners are prudent to protect it from excessive winter dryness and cruel winds. It does not cause allergy problems. Few would dispute that this spruce is far superior to the ubiquitous Norway spruce and deserves

Picea orientalis seed-bearing cones

Picea orientalis pollen-bearing cones

Picea orientalis 'Aureospicata' spring foliage

Picea orientalis 'Connecticut Turnpike'

to be planted more often. Many selections for smaller gardens are available.

'**Atrovirens**': more open than species with exceptionally shiny dark green needles, reaches 60 ft. (18 m) tall.

'**Aureospicata**': new growth comes out butter-yellow in the spring, eye-catching for about six weeks above the previous year's waxy rich dark green foliage.

'**Barnes**': a nestlike bush with a depression in top, slow-growing, shiny dark green needles, reaches 3 ft. (0.9 m) tall by 6 ft. (1.8 m) wide.

'**Bergman's Gem**': cushion-shaped in youth, becoming a flat globe, dense shiny dark green needles.

'**Connecticut Turnpike**': a dense, compact forrm with very dark green needles.

'**Gowdy**': a dense, narrow tree with recurved sweeping branches, pale green new growth in spring becoming dark glossy green.

'**Nana**': a dense, globose form usually not more than 3 ft. (0.9 m) high.

'**Nutans**': a slow-growing, irregular conical form with bright pollen-bearing cones in spring.

'**Skylands**': grows slowly for several years, then 12 to 18 in. (30 to 46 cm) a year, tall and conical, foliage bright yellow year-round with dark green inner needles, needs protection from midday sun in summer. Elegant.

'**Tom Thumb**': dwarf and globose with golden new foliage.

Picea orientalis 'Skylands'

Picea pungens
Colorado spruce
Zones 2 to 6

The Colorado spruce is found in western Montana, Idaho, and the mountains of Colorado south to New Mexico and Arizona. In its native stands it is predominantly green. It is the most planted of the western conifers in the eastern United States.

This dense, pyramidal tree to 60 ft. (18 m) tall by 25 ft. (8 m) wide grows 6 to 12 in. (15 to 30 cm) a year. The needles are sharp and stiff, 1½ in. (3.5 cm) long. They are strongly acidic when chewed. All specimens display a blue cast

Picea orientalis 'Tom Thumb'

or bloom on the foliage, especially on the tips of the new growth of older trees. The seed-bearing cones are tan, pendulous, and 3 to 4 in. (7.5 to 10 cm) long.

Grow this spruce in full sun. It is tolerant of dry sites, wind, air pollution, and salt. It does not thrive in warm, humid areas. The tree is very prone to pests, especially red spider mites, and is also subject to galls. Old plants tend to lose lower branches and become unattractive.

The species itself is not commonly planted because there are so many cultivars with bluer foliage. In fact, selections of this species are some of the bluest of conifers. The intensity of the silvery blue foliage of a few cultivars can be discordant in some plant combinations but is especially attractive when paired with purple or pink flowers. There are sizes and habits for every purpose.

This spruce is readily used as a nest site, especially by robins, mockingbirds, sparrows, purple finches, and mourning doves. In the fall, the seed eaters—crossbills, evening grosbeaks, nuthatches, and goldfinches—congregate for the cone-ripening season. The Colorado spruce is often sold as a holiday tree. It is the state tree of Colorado and Utah.

'**Baby Blueyes**': a dense, symmetrical pyramidal habit, with bright blue foliage, slower growing than 'Hoopsii', faster than 'Montgomery'. Stunning.

'**Blue Pearl**': a compact globe, growing less than 1 in. (2.5 cm) a year, good for trough gardens and miniature railroad landscapes.

'**Compacta**': a dense shrub with horizontal branching and a flat top, forming a graceful spreading skirt with age, blue-green foliage.

'**Fat Albert**': a densely compact, symmetrical form with a broad base and soft silvery blue foliage, reaches 15 ft. (4.5 m) tall.

'**Glauca Compacta**': similar to 'Montgomery'.

'**Globosa**': a compact habit with silvery blue foliage, similar (if not identical) to 'Montgomery'.

'**Hoopsii**': silvery blue foliage sometimes almost white, with long sharp needles, has an irregular shape early on but grows into elegance.

Picea pungens 'Baby Blueyes'

Picea pungens 'Compacta'

Picea pungens 'Hoopsii'

Picea pungens 'Pendula'

'Koster': irregularly shaped in youth, becoming pyramidal, silvery blue foliage, adaptable, small to medium-sized, also listed as 'Kosteri'.

'Montgomery': a compact, broadly pyramidal shrub with silvery blue foliage, grows 3 to 6 in. (7.5 to 15 cm) a year, one of the most common dwarf Colorado spruces, completely mixed up with 'Globosa' in the trade.

'Pendula': variable in cultivation, can be grown as a groundcover or developed into sculptural shapes by staking and training, the growing shoots cascade downward, also known as 'Glauca Pendula'.

'Saint Mary': a rounded mound that does not develop a leader, long blue needles, also listed as 'Saint Mary's Broom'.

'Spring Blast': spring growth creamy white for six weeks, 8 ft. (2.4 m) tall by 4 ft. (1.2 m) wide in ten years.

Picea pungens 'Spring Blast' foliage

Picea pungens 'Montgomery'

Picea pungens 'Spring Ghost'

'**Spring Ghost**': conical habit, creamy white new growth becoming blue-green, reaches 4 ft. (1.2 m) tall in ten years.

'**Thomsen**': bright silver-blue thick needles.

'**Thuem**': compact and mounding, grows slowly to 4 ft. (1.2 m) tall by 3 ft. (0.9 m) wide, powder-blue foliage, also listed as 'Thume'.

'**Walnut Glen**': a compact conical upright habit, gold-tinged gray-blue needles, grows 3 in. (7.5 cm) a year.

PINUS
Pine

Pines are perhaps the most famous of the conifers. Over 100 species of trees and shrubs are distributed throughout the Northern Hemisphere. Three dozen are native to North America, one to Great Britain. *Pinus* is arguably the most wide-ranging and successful genus of trees in North America, rivaled only by *Quercus* (oak) in its ability to grow in a diversity of climates.

Spring "candles" on pines

Clustered needles of pines

Typical pine seed-bearing cone

The principal species of pines are planted extensively in large landscape settings, estates, cemeteries, public areas, and recreational sites. The dwarf selections and those with interesting foliage or branching habits are employed in home settings, mixed borders, and collections. Many pine cultivars have been propagated from witches' brooms, and vary from dense, compact, slow-growing types to large landscape trees.

Description

Pines are usually conical and more or less symmetrical in habit when young, becoming tall and more open-branching and picturesque with age. All are evergreen. The needles are in clusters of usually two, three, or five, depending on the species. This feature is one of the main ways to distinguish among the pines. The foliage color ranges from green to blue-green, and even variegated. The needles are usually long and soft.

The new needle growth is one of the most striking features of pines, emerging like erect candles of very soft tissue, sometimes a different color from the rest of the foliage and in time expanding to normal size and rigidity. Pines make this flush of growth only once a year; when it is over, the tips of the new shoots develop a terminal bud in preparation for the following year's growth. Each year's needles build on the framework set down by the previous. Gardeners often snap off part of the candle before it stretches to create a more compact plant or to shape it into a cloudlike habit. This is commonly referred to as candling. Pines retain their needles for one year to decades, but each year some interior needles will turn brown and fall off (see photo on page 21).

Pines are monoecious. The cones vary in size from narrow and cylindrical to broad and rounded and often hang on the branches for several years. They usually open at maturity, but some remain closed for many years, storing the seeds until a forest fire causes the cones to open. The pollen- and seed-bearing cones are generally easy to distinguish. The bark of pines is typically fissured and scaly with age.

Cultivation

Pines put down deep roots and can grow in hotter and drier areas than other fashionable garden conifers like species of *Abies* (fir), *Chamaecyparis* (falsecypress), or *Picea* (spruce). All pines prefer to grow in full sun, and very few tolerate urban pollution.

Pests and Diseases

White pine blister rust (*Cronartium ribicola*) attacks *Pinus strobus* (eastern white pine) and *P. flexilis* (limber pine), among others. The pathogen has a complicated life cycle with an alternate host genus, *Ribes* (currants and gooseberries); it does not spread pine to pine. The rust, which eventually invades the tree's bark and kills the tree, has spread to most white pine areas in North America. It is an important and troublesome forest pathogen. Many states have quarantines to prevent cultivation of *Ribes* species.

White pine weevil (*Pissodes strobi*) is a destructive native insect that kills the terminal leader of trees growing in full sun. It attacks *Pinus strobus* and sometimes *P. banksiana* (jack pine), *P. densiflora* (Japanese red pine), *P. flexilis*, and *P. sylvestris* (Scots pine). Occasionally it targets *Picea abies* (Norway spruce), *Picea pungens* (Colorado spruce), and *Pseudotsuga menziesii* (Douglas-fir). Gardeners will usually first notice curling, wilting, and dying of the previous year's terminal leader in midsummer.

The larvae of the pine sawfly (*Neodiprion* species) is a common pest on *Pinus banksiana*, *P. densiflora*, *P. sylvestris*, and *P. mugo* (mugo pine). The caterpillar, which has a black head and a green-striped gray-green body, feeds on pine needles and can defoliate entire branches. Sawflies can be removed by hand or hosed off. Chemical sprays are effective when the larvae are small, in early spring.

The larvae of the European (*Rhyacionia buoliana*) and the Zimmerman pine shoot (*Dioryctria zimmermani*) moths feed on the growth tips of two- and three-needled pines, especially *Pinus nigra* (Austrian pine), *P. mugo*, and *P. sylvestris*. These pests kills terminal branches, causing distortions and the production of multiple stems. The injured tips, where the larvae overwinter, should be pruned. Chemicals could be applied as the larvae hatch in the early spring.

Diplodia tip blight (*Sphaeropsis sapinea*; syn. *Diplodia pinea*) causes stunted new shoots with short, brown needles, eventually destroying entire trees. It is perhaps most commonly found on mature individuals of *Pinus nigra* and *P. sylvestris*. Control is difficult. Fallen debris should be removed. Repeated fungicide treatments are sometimes necessary.

Pine needle scale (*Chionaspis pinifoliae*) is oystershell-shaped and can completely cover needles. It especially troubles *Pinus mugo* and *P. sylvestris*. Insecticidal soaps can be effective.

Pine wilt can affect *Pinus densiflora*, *P. nigra*, and *P. sylvestris*. Caused by a nematode, *Bursaphelenchus xylophilus*, the disease enters the bark of a tree as the beetle feeds, often causing a rapid decline and death. Infected trees cannot be successfully treated and should be removed and burned.

Air pollutants like sulfur dioxide and ozone can damage the needles of pines. Highway salt is particularly harmful to *Pinus banksiana*, *P. cembra* (Swiss stone pine), and *P. densiflora*. *Pinus nigra* and *P. thunbergii* (Japanese black pine) are relatively salt-tolerant.

Uses

The seeds of numerous pines are suitable for food. In fact, pines rank near the top of conifers in importance to wildlife. The pine siskin is named after this group of conifers. "Pine nuts" constitute more than 50 percent of the diet of the red crossbill, Clark's nutcracker, and the white-headed woodpecker—an unusual wildlife record. Many other birds and mammals feed on the nutritious, oily seeds to a lesser degree. Several small rodents use the bark as food, and pines are valuable as cover and nesting sites for wildlife.

Pine wood is an important construction and lumber product. Pines also provide resin products, and the branches are popular holiday decorations.

Pinus aristata 'Sherwood Compact'

Pinus aristata 'Sherwood Compact'
Sherwood Compact bristlecone pine
Zones 4 to 7

'Sherwood Compact' is a dense, dwarf, upright selection of *Pinus aristata* (Rocky Mountain bristlecone), a species native to the southwestern United States from Nevada, east to Colorado and south to Arizona. *Pinus aristata* originates in alpine and subalpine forests on dry rocky sites, often in pure stands at higher elevations of 7,500 to 10,000 ft. (2,290 to 3,3050 m). A sharp, slender bristle on the tip of the seed scales gives the pine its common name.

Like the species, 'Sherwood Compact' has an irregular habit and grows very slowly. It is unlikely to reach 4 ft. (1.2 m) after 15 years. The upswept branches have rather stiff, short needles often covered with flecks of sticky dried white resin, which could easily be mistaken for a woolly scale insect infestation. The seed-bearing cone is stalkless. The developing cones are deep purple. The bark is red-brown and becomes shallowly fissured into long irregular ridges.

'Sherwood Compact' requires full sun. It is very tolerant of poor, rocky, and dry soils but grows poorly in hot, humid summers. It is not tolerant of air pollution.

Pinus banksiana
Jack pine
Zones 2 to 6

A member of Captain Cook's expedition, Sir Joseph Banks found a conifer on the east coast of Canada which was subsequently named after him. It is the most widely distributed pine species in North America, and the most northerly as well, reaching far into the tundra. It grows from northern New England and Newfoundland west to Alaska and south into New York, Michigan, Illinois, and Minnesota. It displays great variability in height and habit as it adapts to different sites.

The jack pine is usually a small pyramidal tree from 15 to 40 ft. (4.5 to 12 m) tall, but can be up to 80 ft. (24 m) tall when growing on fertile, sandy locations. More often it develops into a scrubby, stunted tree only 25 ft. (8 m) tall with a crooked trunk, no lower branches, and an irregular crown. Frequently it is a pioneer species, seeding into dry, sandy soils and rocky ridges. The tree can live more than 100 years. It often interbreeds with its cousin, the lodgepole pine (*Pinus contorta*).

The needles are in groups of two, thick, stiff, curved, and twisted, dull dark green, and short, $3/4$ to $1 1/4$ in. (2 to 3 cm) long, persisting for two to three years. The stemless seed-bearing cones are found in forward-pointing clusters of two to four, 1 to $2 1/2$ in. (2.5 to 6 cm) long, dark purple at first, becoming contorted and remaining closed. The cone scales are armed with small, incurved, deciduous prickles. On some trees the mature gray cones remain closed on the tree for up to 20 years, still containing viable seeds. The cones are sealed with resin, which melts only when temperatures are above 120°F (50°C), releasing the seeds. There is a good seed crop every three to four years. Stands of jack pine are reported to burn every 40 to 80 years. The bark is dark brown to black with red tones, ridged and flaky, maturing to a dark grayish brown and furrowed with plates or scales.

This pine is seldom grown as a timber tree because the wood is light, soft, weak, and closely grained. It is used for pulpwood and to some extent for construction. It was once valued by the First Nations peoples for making canoe frames.

Although the jack pine is a very important reforestation species, it cannot be recommended as an ornamental conifer. It often has a short, irregular, and gnarly habit. On the one hand, it appears rumpled. On the other hand, it is a hardy and tough tree, grows rapidly in its youth, and is adaptable to tough sites that are dry or sandy, where it could be used for windbreaks or mass plantings. It is the provincial tree of the Northwest Territories.

'Chippewa': an irregular compact globe with short dark green stiff and twisted needles, grows $1/3$ to $3/4$ in. (0.8 to 2 cm) a year, often used for bonsai or trough gardens.

'Uncle Fogy': a weeping form that is prostrate and sprawls in all directions unless trained, can be grafted to an upright standard, reaches 2 ft. (0.6 m) tall by 15 ft. (4.5 m) wide.

'Wisconsin': a dense globular flat-topped bush, reaches 7 in. (18 cm) tall in ten years.

Pinus banksiana 'Uncle Fogy'

Pinus bungeana bark

Pinus bungeana
Lacebark pine
Zones 5 to 8

The lacebark pine is native to eastern and central China and has long been a favorite planting in temple gardens. It is pyramidal when young, often multistemmed, and has a sparse branching habit, With age it becomes open, flat-topped, and rounded.

The tree grows 6 to 12 in. (15 to 30 cm) a year, eventually reaching 50 ft. (15 m) tall by 30 ft. (9 m) wide. It is extremely slow-growing when young. The foliage is 2 to 4 in. (5 to 10 cm) long. The stiff dark green needles are grouped in threes and appear rather sparse in distribution. They remain on the tree two to four growing seasons. The ferociously spiny seed-bearing cones are oval, 2 to 3 in. (5 to 7.5 cm) long by 1 1/2 in. (3.5 cm) wide. They appear terminally or laterally on the stem and have very short stalks. The bark exfoliates in patches of brown, gray, green, and white after the tree is five to eight years old.

Pinus bungeana is grown for its open habit and showy bark. One could contend that it has the most beautiful bark of any conifer. Place it where it can be viewed throughout the year. The open multistemmed habit will allow filtered light to underplantings, but this characteristic also causes it to break apart under heavy snow loads. While the lacebark pine tolerates wind and drought, it requires good drainage and full sun.

'Silver Ghost': striking silver-gray tones in the bark at an early age.

Pinus cembra
Swiss stone pine
Zones 3 to 7

This formal-looking pine is ideal for smaller landscapes. It is very slow-growing and after 25 years will reach 30 ft. (9 m) high but be only 10 ft. (3 m) wide. The species is native to the central European Alps, northeast Russia, and northern Asia.

The tree is very upright early on, spreading slightly with maturity (like humans). The blue-green needles are 2 to 3 in. (5 to 7.5 cm) long, rather stiff and straight, and densely set with blue-white lines beneath. They remain on the tree up to five years. The stems are thick and covered with dense orange-colored downy hairs. The foliage is flammable.

The short-stalked, 2 to 3½ in. (5 to 9 cm) long cones are terminal, green and globe-shaped in

Pinus cembra

Pinus cembra 'Blue Mound'

the first year and becoming egg-shaped and purple-brown the second year with incurved scales. The cone does not release its seeds until it falls to the ground in the third year. The bark is dark gray and smooth on young trees, eventually developing fissures that expose red-brown and scaly ridges.

The Swiss stone pine is handy for its dense, conical form with branches to the ground. It makes an excellent ornamental with its dense green foliage and uniform growth. Its formal bearing suggests distinct landscape design possibilities. It should be grown in full sun with good drainage. It is very tolerant of wind and salt.

'**Blue Mound**': slower growing than the species, low and mounding reaching 3 ft. (0.9 m) tall by 2 ft. (0.6 m) wide in 16 years, useful for rock gardens.

'**Chalet**': a dense, rounded column of soft bluish green foliage, reaching 5 to 10 ft. (1.5 to 3 m) tall in ten years.

'**Nana**': a slow-growing pyramidal dwarf for small gardens, reaching 24 in. (60 cm) tall in ten years.

'**Stricta**': a slow-growing, dense, narrowly upright form with closely ascending branches.

Pinus densiflora
Japanese red pine
Zones 3 to 7

This hardy native of Japan, Korea, and northeastern China is widely planted as a specimen tree in gardens for its interesting habit and attractive bark. It is drought- and salt-tolerant. The tree can reach 75 ft. (23 m) tall in its native habitat but is much shorter in cultivation. It is usually narrow and conical when young but spreads out in old age, displaying a curved trunk, an irregular habit with rather horizontal branches, and a flat or domed top.

Pinus densiflora is a two-needled pine; the needles remain three years, twisted and soft, 3 to 5 in. (7.5 to 12 cm) long, bright to dark green, displayed upright on the stem. The buds are small and red. The short-stalked cones are small, up to 2 in. (5 cm) long, and often clustered in groups of three to five. They remain on the tree two to three years. The bark is orangish to orange-red and flaking, hence the common name.

Pinus densiflora bark

Pinus densiflora 'Golden Ghost'

The Japanese red pine is particularly popular as a bonsai specimen. It is often used in Asian gardens.

'**Alice Verkade**': a wide-spreading, bun-shaped, multistemmed plant with dense foliage, grows only 3 in. (7.5 cm) a year.

'**Golden Ghost**': beautifully variegated, 6 ft. (1.8 m) tall by 4 ft. (1.2 m) wide in ten years.

Pinus densiflora 'Jane Kluis'

Pinus densiflora 'Oculus-draconis' foliage

'Jane Kluis': a low mounding flat-topped selection, sometimes thought to be a cross with either *Pinus nigra* or *P. thunbergii* (authorities differ), straight stiff needles are held radially around the stem and the buds are prominent, reaches 5 ft. (1.5 m) tall in 20 years.

'Low Glow': a flat, dense dwarf globe with vibrant green needles, reaches 6 ft. (1.8 m) tall.

'Oculus-draconis': needles marked with two yellow bands, reaches 15 ft. (4.5 m) tall by 25 ft. (8 m) wide.

'Pendula': a weeping form, needs to be staked over a standard to display its pendulous character, can be grown as a groundcover and is very effective planted at the top of a wall, down which its branches can cascade.

'Umbraculifera': an upright branching habit with an umbrella-like head, called 'Tanyosho' in Japan, slow-growing, reaches 12 ft. (3.6 m) tall by 20 ft. (6 m) wide in 30 years, older bark ex-

Pinus densiflora 'Pendula' as a groundcover

foliates exposing patterns of red-brown, often grown as a standard.

Pinus flexilis
Limber pine
Zones 4 to 7

The limber pine is a small to medium-sized tree, usually growing 30 to 45 ft. (9 to 14 m) tall, with an open habit. In its native habitat from Alberta (in Canada) through the Rocky Mountains to Colorado and as far south as Arizona (both in the United States), it can reach 70 ft. (21 m) tall. It is a timberline tree, growing at 4,000 to 10,000 feet (1,220 to 3,050 m).

In cultivation the limber pine eventually reaches 50 ft. (15 m) tall with a 35 ft. (10.5 m) spread. It often is multistemmed with straight, vertical trunks and forked, upswept branches. With maturity it becomes broad and flat-topped. The gray-barked branches are frequently long, somewhat twisted, sparsely foliated, and very flexible. The twigs are so flexible that they can be tied into a knot. The blue-green needles are in sheathless bundles of five, $2^1/_2$ to $3^1/_2$ in. (6 to 9 cm) long. The needles are stiff, twisted, and bunched, clasping the tip of the branches, and persist up to six years.

The cones have short stalks and are egg-shaped, 3 to 6 in. (7.5 to 15 cm) long and $1^1/_2$ in. (3.5 cm) wide. They are bright green and ripen to yellow-brown. The basal scales are reflexed and lack bristles. Inside the cones are almost wingless edible seeds. The bark of old trunks is thick, dark gray-brown or almost black and covered with thin, irregular, abundant little scales; younger stems are whitish gray and smooth.

Pinus flexilis should be grown in full sun in well-drained, moist soil. It tolerates wind. Most of the cultivars are grafted.

This species has a symbiotic relationship with the white pine butterfly (*Neopharis menapita*), which feeds upon and spends its entire life span on or near the limber pine. The tree was an important source of construction lumber in earlier times.

'Vanderwolf's Pyramid': considered the best of the blue foliage forms by some, with a dense, uniform habit, 30 to 50 ft. (9 to 15 m) high with a 20 to 30 ft. (6 to 9 m) spread, grows 2 ft. (0.6 m) a year, adaptable to heat and a wide range of soil conditions.

Pinus leucodermis
Bosnian pine
Zones 6 to 8

The Bosnian pine is native to Albania, Bosnia, Macedonia, Serbia, Greece, and Italy. It is a slow-growing, medium-sized tree that reaches 30 ft. (9 m) tall in the garden and 60 to 90 ft. (18 to 27 m) tall in the wild. It takes on a neat, conical outline as a young tree and exhibits medium dense foliage on closely packed and ascending branches. This habit is maintained for many years.

Pinus flexilis 'Vanderwolf's Pyramid'

The erect, rich dark green needles are 2½ in. (6 cm) long and joined in bundles of two. They persist five to six years. The needles are quite stiff, sharply pointed, and usually densely tufted at the ends of the branches. The spring buds are silvery white. The 2 to 3 in. (5 to 7.5 cm) long, egg-shaped seed-bearing cones are blue for one year then turn purplish brown. The lower scale often has an incurved prickle. The cones are in groups of one to three. The bark on young branches is whitish in color, thus the epithet *leucodermis*. The very handsome mature bark is greenish gray in color, sometimes with a little exfoliation.

Grow the Bosnian pine in full sun as a specimen tree in a medium to large garden. It is excellent on dry or shallow chalk soils, the kind of soils found in its native habitat, but it adapts well to landscape culture in well-drained soil. The species is said to be salt-tolerant.

'Compact Gem': a slow-growing dwarf with a slender, dense, compact, conical shape, tolerant of drought and salt.

'Emerald Arrow': a compact spire form with rich dark green foliage on silver branches.

'Iseli Fastigiate': in ten years reaches 15 ft (4.5 m) tall but only 3 ft. (0.9 m) wide, useful for screening.

Pinus leucodermis bark

Pinus leucodermis 'Iseli Fastigiate'

Pinus leucodermis 'Mint Truffle'

'Mint Truffle': develops a dense upright broad teardrop shape with mint-green foliage, reaches 5 to 10 ft. (1.5 to 3 m) tall in ten years.

'Smidtii': a dense, compact mound, grows 1 in. (2.5 cm) a year, also known as 'Schmidtii'.

Pinus mugo
Mugo pine, Swiss mountain pine
Zones 2 to 8

The mugo pine is widely planted and typically shrubby in habit; however, it is a very variable species. It can be a rambling prostrate shrub 2 to 6 ft. (0.6 to 1.8 m) tall or occasionally a small tree to 15 ft. (4.5 m) in the garden. It can reach 30 ft. (9 m) or even higher in its natural habitat in the mountains of central and southern Europe, from Spain to the Balkans. It succeeds in almost all soils.

The needles are 1 to 2 in. (2.5 to 5 cm) long, typically curved or twisted, and in bundles of two, persisting five or more years. The needles are a rich green in well-grown plants but can turn yellowish green in the winter. The seed-bearing cones are stalkless, egg-shaped, 1 to 2 $\frac{1}{2}$ in. (2.5 to 6 cm) long, in groups of one to four. The buds are resinous and red-brown. The bark is gray-brown and scaly. With age there are irregular plates.

Mugo pines prefer full sun with good air circulation in moist to dry, well-drained soil. They can become unattractive in the garden if grown with poor drainage and no air circulation. Mugos tolerate high pH soils. They usually do not produce a single main root and thus are easy to move.

Pinus mugo surrounded by grasses

Pinus mugo 'Mitsch Mini'

Pinus mugo 'Mops' in late autumn

Pinus mugo 'Slowmound'

Pinus mugo is a very important landscape crop species in the United States and is commonly grown as a small specimen plant, often for use in groups in sunny mixed borders or as a foundation planting (remember that nursery specimens can sometimes lack uniformity). It is popular because of its hardiness (zone 2), its adaptability to low fertility in either acid or alkaline soil, and its wind, drought, and heat tolerance. It is best to select a cultivar; many of the more than 130 are very similar to one another. Mugos can be dwarf, upright, or ground-hugging, and have green, gold, or even variegated needles.

'Big Tuna': a dense and compact but broad and upright tree with emerald-green needles, grows 3 to 5 in. (7.5 to 12 cm) a year.

'Corley's Mat': a dwarf, wide-spreading carpeting form with long twisted green needles.

'Gnom': a compact selection with deep jade-green foliage that grows in a dense, globular mound.

'Jakobsen': a flat and spreading selection with thick, somewhat contorted dark green needles, grows 3 in. (7.5 cm) a year.

'Mitsch Mini': one of the best bun-shaped mugos but very slow-growing at 1 in. (2.5 cm) a year, short dark green twisted needles year-round, very salt-tolerant.

'Mops': a formal compact and globose form that reaches 3 ft. (0.9 m) tall, growing about 2 in. (5 cm) a year, resinous bright green needles yellow a bit in winter.

'Ophir': green during the growing season, turning golden in winter, compact and flat-topped, reaching 2 ft. (0.6 m) tall in ten years.

'Sherwood Compact': dwarf, compact, and globe-shaped, growing only 1 to 2 in. (2.5 to 5 cm) a year, a superb choice for rock or trough gardens, dark green year-round with showy buds.

'Slowmound': a dwarf uniform flat carpet of upward-facing shoots, slow-growing.

'Winter Gold': an open shrub with light green twisted needles that turn bright yellow in cold weather, reaches 3 to 5 ft (0.9 to 1.5 m) tall in ten years.

Pinus nigra
Austrian pine
Zones 4 to 7

The Austrian pine is native to eastern and southern Europe, France and Spain to Turkey, Cyprus, and the Ukraine; it is also seen in Morocco and Algeria. It is well adapted to the harsh Mediterranean climate, and in the United States it has naturalized in parts of Illinois. It grows to 120 ft. (36.5 m) tall in its native stands and reaches 60 to 80 ft. (18 to 24 m) tall in cultivation.

Typically broad and conical when young, it becomes flat-topped with a short trunk and low-

Pinus nigra bark

spreading branches as it gets older. The pointed and very stiff needles are 3 to 6 in. (7.5 to 15 cm) long in bundles of two. They are dark green with silvery lines of dots on both surfaces. The needles persist four years or more. The leaf sheath is ½ in. (1.2 cm) long and also persists. The needles do not break cleanly when bent.

The 2 to 4 in. (5 to 10 cm) long, yellow-brown to light brown seed-bearing cones appear in groups of two to four and are stalkless or very short-stalked. The cone scales have thickened tips terminated by a short, blunt spine. They open over the winter and fall in the third spring. The very attractive mature bark of *P. nigra* is fissured with broad flat ridges that are light gray in color with dark brown, nearly black, crevices.

Pinus nigra is a large tree but has little value as a timber tree because the wood is coarse and knotty. It is best grown in full sun in moist, well-

Pinus nigra 'Helga'

drained soils, although in the wild it appears in poor, rocky soils. It is tolerant of most soils (including alkaline soils), wind, salt (all forms are excellent for maritime areas), and urban pollution. It thrives better than any other pine in chalky soils and in bleak exposures and makes an excellent windbreak. In cultivation it is planted as an ornamental and in hedges; it is grown commercially for use as a holiday tree. It is commonly planted in parks and other urban settings because of its dark green leaves which are salt- and pollution-tolerant. Note that there are many subspecies with a great variation in different locations.

'Arnold Sentinel': upright, narrow and conical to 30 ft. (9 m) tall and 6 to 10 ft. (1.8 to 3 m) wide.

'Globosa': a dense plant that reaches 8 ft. (2.5 m) high and wide, often multistemmed with long dark green needles, bark is almost black.

'Helga': a slow-growing, rounded, upright form with bright green needles and white buds.

'Hornibrookiana': a slow-growing dwarf compact shrub with long glossy dark green needles on stout branches, producing cream-colored candles in spring, reaching 3 ft. (0.9 m) tall by 6 ft. (1.8 m) wide in 30 years.

Pinus parviflora
Japanese white pine
Zones 5 to 8

Although pyramidal when young, this native of Japan and Korea becomes open and flat-topped with age. The trunk is often crooked, producing a picturesque plant in maturity. Growing 8 to 18 in. (20 to 46 cm) a year, it can reach 50 ft. (15 m) tall by 35 ft. (10.5 m) wide. The five-to-a-group needles are 1 to 3 in. (2.5 to 7.5 cm) long. They are crowded, curved, twisted, and finely

Pinus parviflora 'Adcock's Dwarf'

toothed, with white bands that give the needles a glaucous appearance. The needles are held for three or four growing seasons. The species produces cones freely on young trees. The cones are 2 to 4 in. (5 to 10 cm) long and very conspicuous on the tree. They open wide when ripe and persist up to six years. The cones are solitary or in clusters, and nearly stalkless, with scales that are larger than those of other five-needled pines. The bark is charcoal-gray with flecks of red and exfoliates with age.

This attractive tree is slow-growing at less than 1 ft. (0.3 m) a year. It is tolerant of most soils but demands good drainage. The Japanese white pine should be grown in full sun or partial shade. It tolerates salt spray but has trouble accepting heat.

Pinus parviflora is useful as a street tree and in containers. This species, very popular for its dwarf and slow-growing cultivars and commonly trained as a bonsai, has been the cause of numerous arguments among botanists; many bonsai trees have been produced on a multitude of different graft understocks, producing dissimilar results, and given invalid cultivar names.

'Adcock's Dwarf': a dense, slow-growing, globose form with short gray-green needles clustered at the branch tips, sometimes varies depending on the understock, reaches 3 to 4 ft. (0.9 to 1.2 m) tall after 25 years.

'Aoba-jo': a narrow fastigiate tree with short curly blue needles.

'Bergman': grows 2 in. (5 cm) a year to produce a broadly conical plant with twisted blue-green needles, pollen-bearing cones are bright red in the spring.

'Brevifolia': a small tree with sparse open branching and tight bundles of short blue-green needles.

Pinus parviflora 'Goldilocks'

Pinus parviflora 'Ogon Janome' foliage

'Glauca Nana': extremely slow-growing with an open habit, eventually becomes a flat-topped globe with short, twisted, blue needles.

'Goldilocks': a small cushion with bright gold leaves that burn in full sun.

'Ogon Janome': one of the dragon's-eye pines, this one with bands of distinctive bright golden yellow bands on green needles.

'Tani-mano-uki': slow-growing with creamy white needles that benefit from some protection.

Pinus strobus
Eastern white pine, Weymouth pine
Zones 3 to 7

Without disturbance, an eastern white pine can grow for as along as 400 years. It is the tallest tree native to eastern North America, the state tree of Maine and Michigan, and the provincial tree of Ontario. It once grew in vast forests across the continent. The trees, marvelously straight and thick, were 150 ft. (46 m) tall, with 80 ft. (24 m) or more of the trunk free of branches.

No other tree has played so great a role in the life and history of the people of North America. It spawned the forest industry: navy fleets were built with it, settlements grew up around the sawmills, and railroads and canals were constructed to move the pine from the forests. Native peoples used the bark, needles, and gum to treat lung problems, and even modern cough syrups contain ingredients derived from it.

Pinus strobus is widespread from Newfoundland west to southeastern Manitoba and south into northern Georgia. It often is found growing in pure stands on well-drained sandy soils. In cultivation, it grows best in a rich moist soil in full sun. It is not tolerant of salt, air pollution, ozone, or sulfur dioxide and should not be planted close to highways. It also does not tolerate clay soil. It is easily transplanted because of its wide-spreading root system.

The tree grows 1 to 3 ft. (0.3 to 0.9 m) a year. It is pyramidal when young, and open and spreading with age, often becoming flat-topped and irregular. It typically develops a single central trunk and seldom needs any pruning but does require plenty of open space for adequate root development. Pines are very flammable.

This very handsome and ornamental species is a valuable plant for parks, estates, and other large properties. It is one of the most beautiful pines native to North America. In England it is known as the Weymouth pine (after Lord Weymouth, who planted it in Wiltshire in the early 18th century), but it does not do as well in that climate. A well-grown mature white pine is without equal. Unfortunately this imposing tree is often placed in spaces too small for it to achieve its potential.

The bluish green needles are in groups of five, up to 5 in. (12 cm) long. They are soft, thin, straight, and flexible and held for two seasons. The buds are small, pointed, and resinous. The late summer and autumn browning and shedding of the older needles is entirely natural. Needles develop only toward the ends of the twigs. The cones are cylindrical, 4 to 6 in. (10 to 15 cm) long; they take two years to mature and hang from a thick, short, round stem. Trees begin bearing cones at age five to ten and produce heavily every three to five years. The cones are aromatic and often ooze white resin. The bark on older trees is dark gray-brown, rough, and furrowed, 1 to 2 in. (2.5 to 5 cm) thick. The smooth, thin bark of young trees is damaged easily by fire or by careless use of string trimmers.

Dwarf forms of *Pinus strobus* can be very confusing. The same plant often appears under several names (for instance, 'Nana' is frequently labeled 'Umbraculifera'). The cultivars 'Radiata', 'Blue Shag', 'Pumila', 'Compacta', and 'Umbraculifera' can be differentiated only by an expert. The same is true of the faster growing 'Pygmaea' and 'UConn' as well as the dwarfs 'Horsford', 'Minuta', and 'Sea Urchin'.

'Blue Shag': slow-growing, 4 in. (10 cm) a year with a dense, rounded habit and silver-blue needles.

'Coney Island': dense foliage that is tufted at the ends of the branches with a cloudlike form wider than tall, growing 3 in. (7.5 cm) a year to 3 ft. (0.9 m) tall by 5 ft. (1.5 m) wide, producing many small cones.

'Contorta': densely set twisted branches and leaves.

Pinus strobus bark

Pinus strobus 'Contorta'

PINUS STROBUS

'Fastigiata': branches ascend at a 45° angle from the trunk, beautiful fast-growing, narrowly upright cultivar, drought-tolerant, adaptable to a wide range of growing conditions, less likely than the species to lose branches from ice and snow. An excellent choice, especially for smaller properties. Should be used more in eastern North America.

'Horsford': one of the best bun-shaped dwarf pines, seldom reaches 5 ft. (1.5 m) tall and wide,

Pinus strobus 'Fastigiata'

Pinus strobus 'Louie'

Pinus strobus 'Minuta'

Pinus sylvestris foliage and pollen-bearing cones

Pinus sylvestris seed-bearing cones

grows 2 in. (5 cm) a year, has thin, medium green needles, produces cones early.

   'Louie': golden needles in all seasons.

   'Merrimack': a dense, compact, rounded globe of silver-blue foliage growing 4 in. (10 cm) a year to 8 ft. (2.5 m) tall.

   'Minuta': a low-growing compact bun with short blue-green needles, reaching 5 ft. (1.5 m) tall after 20 years, does not produce cones, questionably legitimate name.

   'Pendula': often multistemmed and irregular in form, the branches are horizontal with the branchlets pendulous, reaches 10 ft. (3 m) tall and wide, can be a living sculpture with its large clusters of long, twisting, graceful blue-green needles. Old specimens are wonders to behold.

   'Radiata': slow-growing and globose, to 4 ft. (1.2 m) tall after 25 years, often labeled 'Nana'.

   'Sea Urchin': thin but dense blue needles on a low mounded plant that grows only 2 in. (5 cm) a year to 3 to 4 ft. (0.9 to 1.2 m) tall and wide.

   'Torulosa': a weird, open, upright form with twisted branches and densely set, twisted needles.

   'UConn': an upright, broad, dense, compact, flat-topped selection that reaches 18 ft. (5.5 m) tall in 15 years, maintains a nice form without shearing.

Pinus sylvestris
Scots pine, Scotch pine
Zones 2 to 8

The Scots pine is the only pine native to the British Isles. Once common throughout England and Wales, the species is still encountered in wild stands in northern Scotland. It is established in most of Europe and Asia from Spain north and east as far as Siberia and south into Turkey, making it one of the most widely distributed and hardiest pines in the world. It also is one of the most

Pinus sylvestris 'Globosa Viridis'

important timber trees in those regions. Since its introduction in 1752, it has naturalized in North America from southeastern Canada and New England west to Iowa.

The Scots pine typically grows 30 to 60 ft. (9 to 18 m) tall but can be up to 90 ft. (27 m) tall. Young plants are conical, but with age become high-branched, flat-topped, or umbrella-shaped. Some plants develop a gnarled, interesting shape. The needles are 1½ to 3 in. (3.5 to 7.5 cm) long, twisted, rigid, and in twos. The foliage is a glaucous blue-green with waxy white lines on both surfaces, persisting for three years.

The pollen-bearing cones are yellow, clustered at the base of the current season's shoots. Dark red seed-bearing cones develop at the tips of the current season's shoots. The cones appear singly or in groups of two or three. They are only 1 to 3 in. (2.5 to 7.5 cm) long, short-stalked, and usually point backward on the branch. The cone scales are often flat and quite thick at the tip. There are no prickles on the back of the cone.

The mature bark is gray or red-brown with long fissures. Stems up to 12 in. (30 cm) in diameter have a thin orange bark (light to dark brown, reddish, or cinnamon) that exfoliates in small, irregular papery plates. The bark is very attractive and noticeable, since the trees so often are high branched.

Grow this pine in full sun on acidic, well-drained soils. It tolerates a wide range of soil conditions, including poor soil, and will seed into poor sandy soils where it can outgrow other species. It is very tolerant of moisture and climatic extremes.

The Scots pine is an important holiday tree because of its rapid growth during youth and because of its blue-green foliage. With its resistance to urban smog, its hardiness, and its adaptability, it is also useful for windbreaks and screens. It is not a good choice for zones 7 or 8, however, as it is intolerant of heat and drought. It is striking with its bright orange-red peeling bark when young and its cones that point backward along the branches.

'**Albyns**': a slow-growing, prostrate form 8 ft. (2.5 m) wide by only 16 in. (40 cm) tall, with thick shiny needles year-round. Good as a groundcover.

'**Aurea**': foliage that turns golden yellow in early winter and is blue-green with a hint of yellow during the warm seasons, growing slowly to 30 to 50 ft. (9 to 15 m) tall.

'**Beuvronensis**': a broad, low, bushy, dome-shaped form with blue-green needles, grows very slowly to 4 ft. (1.2 m) tall after decades. Ideal for rock gardens.

'**Globosa Viridis**': an ovoid shrub that is densely clothed to the ground with long, shaggy, mid-green foliage, a knobby appearance, sometimes listed as *Pinus nigra*.

'**Hillside Creeper**': grows 12 in. (30 cm) a year to form a large mat of undulating branches with medium green needles. A strong grower.

'**Watereri**': usually considered a dwarf plant with a globose form, only 8 to 12 in. (20 to 30 cm) tall and wide, but it can grow 4 to 6 in. (10 to 15 cm) a year to 12 ft. (3.6 m) tall, foliage appears blue.

Pinus sylvestris 'Watereri'

Pinus thunbergii
Japanese black pine
Zones 5 to 10

The Japanese black pine is native to Japan and Korea, where it is often found growing along the seacoast. The habit is often fairly symmetrical but with a curved trunk. This pine grows 8 to 12 in. (20 to 30 cm) a year to 50 ft. (15 m) tall and half as wide. The dark green, sharply pointed needles are stiff, 4 to 6 in. (10 to 15 cm) long, in bundles of two. They persist for three to five years. The buds are covered with silky white hairs, a simple heat and drought tolerance but demands full sun. It commonly breaks apart in ice and snow storms.

The Japanese black pine is very popular in Asian gardens, where it is typically trained to create the appearance of ancient wild trees. It is also a popular subject for bonsai. This species is one of the most important timber trees in Japan. It has been planted to stabilize sand dunes.

'**Banshosho**': becomes dense and globose with rich green foliage.

'**Oculus-draconis**' (dragon's-eye black pine): irregularly shaped, named for the green needles with yellow-white stripes that are said to resemble a dragon's eye, a feature most apparent in the fall.

'**Thunderhead**': a broadly spreading, irregularly branched dwarf that reaches 8 ft. (2.5 m) tall by 10 ft. (3 m) wide after ten years, displays clusters of distinctive silver-white buds and candles against rich dark green, densely packed needles in early spring.

Pinus thunbergii 'Oculus-draconis'

Pinus thunbergii 'Thunderhead' candles

way to identify this species. The fissured bark is charcoal-gray. The cones are 1½ to 2½ in. (3.5 to 6 cm) long and short-stalked with prickly scales; they are solitary or carried in clusters.

This pine grows in any well-drained soil. It tolerates salt spray and salt in soil. It has great

Pinus wallichiana
Himalayan pine
Zones 5 to 7

This handsome pine is used in much the same way as *Pinus strobus* and has the same cultural requirements; however, it grows a tad slower and can be a bit more broad. It is native to the Himalayas, from Afghanistan to Nepal. Danish surgeon Nathaniel Wallich (1786–1854), who is commemorated in the epithet, was a botanist with the East India Company and superintendent of the Calcutta Botanic Garden. He introduced this plant from his travels into England in 1823. It has also been known as *P. griffithii*.

This conifer can reach 80 ft. (24 m) tall in cultivation and tends to be wide-spreading. Older specimens usually retain their lower branches; however, they can become tattered and shabby in old age. The tree benefits from a sheltered position.

The Himalayan pine exhibits great grace, owing to the feathery effect of the 6 to 8 in. (15 to 20 cm) long needles; these are in clusters of five and

Pinus wallichiana 'Zebrina' foliage

persist for three to four years. They appear bent, and most of the needle is pendulous. The grayish green to blue-green foliage has a soft appearance. The solitary seed-bearing cones are up to 10 in. (25 cm) long and hang on a long 1 to 2 in. (2.5 to 5 cm) stalk. They are very resinous.

'Nana': a dwarf and congested selection with short silver needles.

'Zebrina': graceful downward-hanging needles are banded with a yellow stripe, needs winter protection, sometimes labeled 'Oculus-draconis'.

Pseudolarix amabilis
Golden-larch
Zones 4 to 7

This monotypic genus is native to the mountains of eastern China. The species is a deciduous conifer like the larch (*Larix*) but it is not a true larch. Some consider the foliage of the golden-larch the most eye-catching of any conifer (see page 8). In fact, the epithet *amabilis* means "worthy of love," and the burnt-orange fall color is the glory of this plant. Unfortunately, like many love affairs, this fall display is brief.

The mint-green leaves emerge in early spring and unfold into soft, feathery, flat needles. They are in whorls of 15 to 30, and the length of the individual needles varies from 1 to 2½ in. (2.5 to 6 cm) long. The clusters of needles are arranged spirally, widely spaced on spur shoots that are noticeably longer than those of *Larix*. There is a distinct constriction between the annual rings. The leaves turn a dazzling golden orange in the fall, appearing as if lighted from within.

The pollen-bearing cones are catkinlike in clusters. The seed-bearing cones mature in one year on the upper side of the branch, are in the form of rosettes with pointed triangular scales resembling artichokes. These cones may be up to 2½ in. (6 cm) long and are blue-green maturing to golden brown. The ripe cones disintegrate and release the winged seeds, and the thick cone scales fall to the ground. The bark is charcoal-gray.

The tree reaches 40 to 70 ft. (12 to 21 m) tall by 50 ft. (15 m) wide in the landscape, perhaps taller in the wild. It has a pyramidal habit with ascending limbs, and the open nature of the foliage makes some underplanting possible. It is very slow-growing. A six-year-old seedling will be only 9 ft. (2.7 m) tall. A 100-year-old specimen was reported to be 45 ft. (14 m) tall.

The golden-larch does best in full sun, although it tolerates light shade. It does best in fertile, well-drained moist soil. The tree, which is said to be tolerant of summer heat and humidity, grows successfully in the southeastern United States, where most true larches and firs do poorly; however, one would be wise to protect it from harsh winter winds. It does not like limestone soil.

This species is difficult to propagate (it seldom produces viable seed unless growing in a grove, and cuttings do not root) and is therefore hard to find in nurseries; but this does not daunt collectors. It has also been called *Pseudolarix kaempferi*. The wood has been used for furniture, boat-building, and bridges.

Pseudotsuga menziesii
Douglas-fir
Zones 4 to 7

The Douglas-fir is native from British Columbia south to Washington, Oregon, and California and eastward into Idaho, Montana, Wyoming, Utah, Colorado, Arizona, and New Mexico. It is not actually a fir or even in the same family as the true firs (*Abies*). In the wild with abundant rainfall and mild winters it can reach 225 ft. (68 m) tall with almost half that height free of branches. Specimens have been recorded at well over 300 ft. (90 m) in height, making the Douglas-fir the largest conifer in the world except for the coast redwoods of California. It can live up to a thousand years. There are several geographic varieties.

Pseudotsuga menziesii is a pioneer species, frequently colonizing areas that have been subjected to wildfires or logging. While it develops best in full sun, it does tolerate some shade and it can do well in a wide range of climatic conditions. It prefers deep, well-drained, sandy loams with plentiful moisture. This conifer is tough and durable, but it would be wise to avoid planting it in the dry, windy sections of the midwestern United States.

In the landscape it will grow 40 to 80 ft. (12 to 24 m) tall. The habit is dense and conical; if crowded, however, the habit is spirelike. The branches sweep downward. The root system is strong and wide-spreading.

Through the years this species has been referred to as a spruce and a pine as well as a fir and hemlock. This is very understandable if only the foliage is examined. The ¾ to 1¼ in. (2 to 3 cm) long needles are held singly and are flat, with a row of white dots on the bottom. The needles are arranged spirally around the stem, are a dark

Pseudolarix amabilis fall foliage

Pseudotsuga menziesii seed-bearing cone

blue-green with a brighter spring growth, and remain on the tree for four to eight years.

Since the needles cannot be used for accurate identification of this conifer, one should look at the buds. They are an easy ID feature for this species; they are long, shiny, covered with chestnut-brown overlapping scales, and pointed.

The pollen-bearing cones are catkinlike, yellow to orange-red, and pendulous. The stalked 2 to 4 in. (5 to 10 cm) long seed-bearing cones are egg-shaped and dark brown with long extruded, three-forked, pointed papery bracts between the scales of the cones. These cones mature in the first autumn and drop intact after the seeds are dispersed. The red-brown bark is deeply furrowed and thickens with age. In youth it is gray and smooth with resin blisters.

The entire northwestern United States was once a vast forest of Douglas-fir. This species became the world's most important timber tree source when the towering white pines of the eastern United States were exhausted by the end of the nineteenth century. The Douglas-fir was used for telephone and telegraph poles and railroad ties, and is now used for all sorts of construction and for plywood manufacture. The wood is resistant to decay, does not warp, and is stronger for its weight than any other native tree. Since the trees are so large, it is possible to produce very large beams for use in building bridges, docks, and large structures. The Douglas-fir is commonly grown as a holiday tree because the needles remain on the tree long after it is cut. The seeds are an important food source for wildlife, including squirrels, chipmunks, crossbills, nutcrackers, and juncos.

A mature specimen is appropriate for a large estate, commercial area, or arboretum. It is not suitable for a small residential garden. The Douglas-fir is the state tree of Oregon.

'Fastigiata': narrow with short upright branches, reaches 40 ft. (12 m) tall with a 10 to 15 ft. (3 to 4.5 m) spread, dense, useful for screen planting.

'Graceful Grace': fast-growing with long blue-green needles, irregular upright leader, lateral branches drooping, does not need staking.

'Pendula': slow-growing, crown pendulous and irregular.

'Pumila': shrub form.

Pseudotsuga menziesii 'Pendula'

Pseudotsuga menziesii 'Pumila'

Sciadopitys verticillata
Umbrella-pine
Zones 5 to 8

The umbrella-pine (not actually a pine) is native to southern Japan. It is the sole species in this genus and has a history dating back to the dinosaurs. In the wild it has been observed over 100 ft. (30 m) tall. In cultivation it is more likely to reach 30 ft. (9 m) by half as wide.

Sciadopitys verticillata is usually grown as a feature plant by connoisseurs or in collections. It prefers rich, moist soils in full sun with protection from high winds. It does grow in part shade but dislikes lime soils. It is very slow-growing in youth.

This conifer is often multistemmed and matures into a dense and conical tree with ascending upper branches. The stems are light brown. The foliage is luxuriant. The 3 to 5 in. (7.5 to 12 cm) long needles are displayed on orange-brown shoots in whorls of 10 to 30, like the spokes of an

Sciadopitys verticillata 'Joe Kozey'

Sciadopitys verticillata foliage

umbrella. They are fleshy and pliable. The upper surface is glossy dark green but paler beneath with a center groove on both surfaces (actually two needles fused in pairs). The foliage yellows in winter in cold climates.

The pollen-bearing cones are in dense clusters arranged spirally at the tip of branches. The solitary green seed-bearing cones are 2 to 4 in. (5 to 10 cm) long on short stalks and mature to brown in the second year. The handsome bark is red-brown and peels in long strips.

Hoofed browsers will select the umbrella-pine over more common species. The spicy scented wood is water-resistant and used for boat-building.

'Golden Rush': foliage a good golden color, also listed as 'Gold Rush'.

'Grüne Kugel': a multibranched dwarf.

'Joe Kozey': a columnar habit with dominant leader and rich green foliage, reaches 6 ft. (1.8 m) tall by 3 ft. (0.9 m) wide in ten years.

'Ossorio Gold': golden yellow needles, upright cones, grows 4 ft. (1.2 m) tall by 3 ft. (0.9 m) wide in ten years, rare and prized.

'Sternschnuppe': upright and narrow with short thick branches and needles, 4 ft. (1.2 m) tall by 2 ft. (0.6 m) wide in ten years.

'Wintergreen': a narrow conical habit with deep green foliage that does not yellow in winter, grows 9 in. (23 cm) a year, better for colder climates.

Sciadopitys verticillata 'Ossorio Gold'

Sciadopitys verticillata 'Wintergreen'

Sequoiadendron giganteum
Giant sequoia, Sierra redwood
Zones 6 to 8

This large tree with a massive fluted trunk and thick bark is found in groves on the western slopes of the Sierra Nevada in California. There it thrives in cool autumn mists and deep winter snows followed by dry summers. The giant sequoia is the world's largest tree in terms of mass (volume). Heights up to 350 ft. (106 m) have been claimed. In cultivation it is likely to reach 60 ft. (18 m) tall.

Younger trees have a pyramidal shape with branches that droop at the ends. When grown in the open as a garden specimen, the branches are retained to the ground. After a century of growth, the trees are tall and straight and clear of branches with a high crown.

The tiny blue-green leaves, $1/8$ to $1/4$ in. (0.3 to 0.6 cm) long, are awl-shaped and sharp and arranged spirally on the stem, overlapping and tightly appressed to it, lending a cordlike appearance. The needles persist for four years. The stalked cone is absurdly small, $1 1/2$ to 2

Sequoiadendron giganteum

SEQUOIADENDRON GIGANTEUM

in. (3.5 to 5 cm) long, for so large a tree. It has thick woody scales that are swollen at the edge. The cones mature from green to brown the second season and persist on the tree for several years.

The spongy bark is a rich red-brown and is said to be up to 12 in. (30 cm) thick, or even thicker on mature specimens, with deep furrows and fibrous ridges. The sap is high in tannic acid, which is claimed to protect the tree from fire damage and to aid in wound healing. The bark is soft and easily hollowed out by birds and squirrels. This tree does not sucker.

The giant sequoia is striking with its huge red trunk and neat pyramidal shape. Logged trees have been recorded at more than three thousand years old. The species is widely planted through Europe and is especially popular in Great Britain and Germany. Redwood, which includes *Sequoiadendron giganteum* and *Sequoia sempervirens*, is the state tree of California.

'**Blauer Eichzwerg**': slow-growing pyramidal miniature, blue foliage, reaches 3 ft. (0.9 m) tall in ten years. Ideal for miniature railroad landscapes or rock gardens.

'**Glaucum**': narrow habit, slower growing than species, bright blue foliage.

'**Hazel Smith**': selected for hardiness to zone 6, uniformly pyramidal, blue-green compared to species, grows 18 in. (46 cm) a year.

Sequoiadendron giganteum bark

Sequoiadendron giganteum 'Hazel Smith'

'Pendulum': tall pillar with branches completely pendulous and parallel with trunk, sometimes leaning this way and that, with upward branches contorted, growing upright, then dipping and growing upright again, often multiple leaders. Freaky.

TAXODIUM
Bald-cypress, pond-cypress

The two species of this genus are now found naturally only in eastern North America; however, in the past they were much more widely distributed. Both plants have alternately arranged deciduous foli-

Sequoiadendron giganteum 'Pendulum'

age that is a pale yellow-green. Both will grow in very wet conditions and produce large buttressed trunks, sometimes generating peculiar kneelike projections. The "knees" are roots that come above the surface of the soil and are thought to help anchor the tree; they form only in wet habitats.

Taxodium ascendens
Pond-cypress
Zones 5 to 10

Many authorities list this as *Taxodium distichum* var. *nutans*. The pond-cypress is found in swampy areas and pine barrens from southeast-

Taxodium ascendens fall color

Taxodium distichum
Bald-cypress
Zones 4 to 11

This large tree is found in swamps from the coastal plain of Delaware to Florida, west to Texas, and up the Mississippi Valley to Illinois and Indiana. It often reaches 100 ft. (30 m) in height in its native stands; in cultivation it is more likely to be 50 ft. (15 m) at maturity. It sometimes lives a thousand years or more. It is pyramidal when young, becoming more rounded as it ages. Mature trees have flat-topped crowns; Spanish moss drapes from their branches in the southern United States.

The bald-cypress requires full sun and acidic soil to thrive. It does best in moist, deep soil with good drainage but will grow in standing water and is also tolerant of dry soil. Of all trees it has probably the greatest known tolerance for flooding; some specimens are in standing water half of the growing season. It is a tough and adaptable species.

The buds are tiny, roundish, and alternately arranged. The sage-green deciduous leaves are $1/2$ to $3/4$ in. (1.2 to 2 cm) long, in a flat, featherlike arrangement in two rows on narrow branchlets. The autumn color is russet or a soft brown. The leaves drop from the tree to form a carpet of soft needles. The pollen-bearing cones appear in winter; they are catkinlike, in 4 to 5 in. (10 to 12 cm) long drooping terminal panicles in early to mid spring. The seed-bearing cones are $3/4$ to 1 in. (2 to 2.5 cm) in diameter, globular, appearing singly or in pairs at the end of twigs.

The trunk is straight and buttressed at the base. The bark is fibrous, reddish brown, and peels off in thin, narrow strips. Its roots form natural crooks or knees that extend above ground when it is grown near water. This species has knees more sharply pointed than those of the pond-cypress.

This is an important timber species. The wood is very durable and is used for construction of objects that will be exposed to water: boats, docks, bridges, greenhouses, crates, railroad ties, and houses for livestock and birds.

Taxodium ascendens foliage

ern Virginia to Florida and west to Louisiana. It has a slow to medium growth rate, commonly reaching 80 ft. (24 m) tall by 20 ft. (6 m) wide, although ultimate heights of as much as 125 ft. (38 m) are possible.

The habit is narrowly conical or columnar. The deciduous branchlets ascend rigidly from the twig rather than spreading out. The leaves are $1/8$ to $5/8$ in. (0.3 to 1.5 cm) long, narrow, and spirally arranged in a plane closely held against the twigs; they appear scalelike on the branchlets. The foliage is bright green in the summer and turns orange-brown in fall. The pollen-bearing cones are in drooping terminal panicles. The seed-bearing cones are $1/2$ to $1 1/4$ in. (1.2 to 3 cm) round on short stalks. The bark is ridged and deeply furrowed with long vertical plates.

This species does not develop knees as readily as *Taxodium distichum*. The pond-cypress is adaptable and wind-tolerant.

'Nutans': slow-growing, columnar habit, young foliage somewhat pendulous on the erect branchlets.

'Prairie Sentinel': a tall narrow habit with shorter branches than the species, reaches 60 ft. (18 m) tall by 10 ft. (3 m) wide.

Taxodium distichum "knees"

Taxodium distichum seed-bearing cones

Taxodium distichum 'Cascade Falls'

Taxodium distichum 'Secrest'

TAXODIUM DISTICHUM

The number of mature bald-cypresses is declining because of the widespread draining of swamplands. It is the state tree of Louisiana.

'Cascade Falls': a pendulous large shrub or small tree not exceeding 20 ft. (6 m) in height, sage-green foliage, red-brown bark, russet fall color.

'Peve Minaret': spire-shaped, fine-textured overlapping needles, bright green in summer turning rusty red in fall, reaches 12 ft. (3.6 m) tall by 3 ft. (0.9 m) in ten years,

'Peve Yellow': similar to 'Peve Minaret' but with fine-textured soft yellow foliage, turning orange and reddish in fall, sometimes irregular growth early on but becomes open.

'Secrest': globose, flat-topped, grows 3 to 6 in. (7.5 to 15 cm) a year to 6 ft. (1.8 m) tall.

Taxodium distichum 'Peve Minaret'

Taxodium distichum 'Peve Yellow'

TAXUS
Yew

Taxus comprises about ten similar species. Three are native to North America and one to England. Many selections from these species are used in public landscaping and in both estate and home gardens. The plants vary from low and wide-spreading to tall and columnar. Many of the cultivars are similar and difficult to single out one from another.

Description

Yews can be shrubs or trees to 70 ft. (21 m) tall and can live for hundreds of years. They usually display an irregular crown and are often broad-spreading. The flat evergreen needles are single and arranged spirally or in a flat plane, often appearing to be two-ranked, with the edge of the leaf often slightly curled. The tip of the needle is sharp and pointed. The needles remain on the tree for up to eight years. Growth is vigorous in the spring with side shoots on the new growth.

Yews are dioecious. The pollen-bearing cones are small and yellow on the underside of the previous year's growth. The seed-bearing cones mature in autumn, with the single seed embedded in a bright red aril (a fleshy pulp that is open at the apex).

Taxus baccata, a 300-year-old tree

The bark is reddish to dark chestnut-brown and exfoliates from the trunk and larger branches in long, thin strips.

ID Features
Whether the leaf tip is abruptly pointed or not is an ID feature among some yews.

Cultivation
Yews tolerate considerable shade but do best in full sun. They also adapt to most well-drained soils but not wet conditions or extreme heat. They can be trimmed and shaped into hedges or topiaries and tolerate urban pollution but not salt.

Taxus bark

Taxus topiary

Uses

The foliage, bark, and seeds are very poisonous to farm livestock, but not to moose, elk, or deer. The fleshy red aril that surrounds the seeds is not poisonous. Birds eat the arils and spread the seed. The wood of yews is very durable. Yews are a symbol of immortality, and over the centuries have been widely planted in cemeteries.

Taxus baccata
English yew, common yew
Zones 6 to 8

The English yew is native to Europe, northern Africa, and southwestern Asia. It is one of Britain's three native conifers (many magnificent specimens can be seen there, some thousands of years old) and was planted in New Jersey as early as 1713.

It is a dense, wide-spreading tree, growing 30 to 60 ft. (9 to 18 m) tall, with a thick trunk; however, it is often grown with multiple trunks. The very dark green to black-green needles are ½ to 1½ in. (1.2 to 3.5 cm) long; they gradually taper to a point. They are convex with a prominent midrib and are usually spirally arranged. The pollen-bearing cones are inconspicuous.

Taxus baccata 'David'

Taxus baccata seed-bearing cones

The seed-bearing cones are ½ in. (1.2 cm) long and coral-red. The bark is reddish brown and furrowed; older trunks become fluted.

This yew must have well-drained soils but is remarkably tolerant of shade and is easy to transplant. It grows 8 in. (20 cm) a year.

The wood makes excellent firewood and can be used for furniture, tool handles, and bows. It is claimed that Robin Hood made his weapons from this wood and was married under a yew as well as buried beneath one. The English yew is most often seen trimmed into dense hedges and screens or shaped into topiary and used on large estates.

Although the species is not often found, many narrow, upright cultivars are available as well as hardier crosses (*Taxus* ×*media*) with the Japanese yew (*T. cuspidata*).

'**Amersfoort**': a slow-growing open shrub with rigid upright branches, needles arranged radially, flat oval leaves look a bit like boxwood, reaches 4 ft. (1.2 m) high and 2 ft. (0.6 m) wide in ten years, tolerates full shade and dry conditions, dislikes wet soil.

'**David**': an upright form with yellow needles.

'**Dovastonii Aurea**': a slow-growing large bush to small tree with wide-spreading branches and golden yellow pendulous tips, retains color in shade, 20 in. (50 cm) high by 4 ft. (1.2 m) wide in ten years, male.

'**Fastigiata Robusta**': vigorous and upright, leaves lighter green.

'**Repandens**': prostrate and wide-spreading with pendulous branch tips, seldom exceeds 4 ft. (1.2 m) tall but can spread to 15 ft. (4.5 m) across in time, dense, glossy black-green foliage, tolerates shady conditions, can be shaped easily, female, hardy to zone 5.

'**Semperaurea**': slow-growing, wide-spreading, golden yellow color retained year-round even in semi-shade, trims well, male.

Taxus baccata 'Repandens'

'**Standishii**': slow-growing dense column of tightly packed branches, golden yellow foliage, female.

Taxus cuspidata
Japanese yew
Zones 4 to 7

The Japanese yew is native to Japan, Korea, and China. The small tree has an irregular habit and can reach 40 ft. (12 m) tall, but most garden selections are shrub-sized. The ½ to 1 in. (1.2 to 2.5 cm) long foliage is irregularly arranged, a dark lustrous green with yellow-green bands on the underside. The apex is abruptly sharp-pointed. The seed-bearing cone is a red aril.

The Japanese yew is perhaps the hardiest and fastest-growing yew, and the easiest to cultivate. It prefers moist, well-drained, sandy, slightly acidic soil in sun or shade. It is a common ornamental in Japan, where the wood has been used for construction, carving, bathtubs, chopsticks, clogs, and bows. In the West it is useful for groundcovers, foundation planting, and hedging.

Taxus cuspidata is hardier than *T. baccata* and is often crossed with that species, resulting in *T.* ×*media*. This makes the correct naming of some cultivars difficult.

Taxus baccata 'Standishii'

Taxus cuspidata 'Aurescens'

'**Aurescens**': low-growing, compact, can be wide-spreading, small needles with yellow new growth, shade-tolerant, seldom exceeds 3 ft. (0.9 m) tall and wide, avoid wet sites.

Taxus ×media
Hybrid yew
Zones 4 to 7(8)

This very common hybrid between *Taxus baccata* and *T. cuspidata* has many similar cultivars. It is valued for its hardiness and vigor, and its shade tolerance, which it inherits from its Japanese parent, *T. cuspidata*. The growth characteristics of these hybrids can vary widely; most selections are shrubby, from 2 to 20 ft. (0.6 to 6 m) tall. The pointed needles are usually two-ranked; they are dark green with a lighter underside. The fleshy red aril encloses a single seed. The bark is brown and scaly. Hybrid yews are indispensable for use in foundation and mass plantings and as screens and hedges.

'**Beanpole**': a very narrow, 8 in. (20 cm) tall, dense, fastigiate form, slow-growing, female.

'**Flushing**': an upright, narrow, columnar form with glossy dark green foliage and bright red cones, reaches 12 to 15 ft. (3.6 to 4.5 m) tall but only 3 ft. (0.9 m) wide, female.

'**Halleri**': fast-growing and erect, male.

'**Hicksii**': fast-growing and erect with shiny rich green needles, can reach 20 ft. (6 m) tall after many years but usually pruned, excellent for hedging, usually female.

THUJA
Arborvitae

Thuja is a small genus of six species from Asia and North America found in moist forests and on the banks of streams. Valued as ornamental plants in landscapes of every size, they are widely used in public spaces and private gardens for screening and foundation plantings or as specimens. They grow without much attention and are among the most versatile and easy-to-grow conifers that adapt to colder northern landscapes. In the United States, the splendor of the western native

Taxus ×media 'Beanpole'

T. plicata has not been fully appreciated in the eastern half of the country.

Description

The foliage is usually scalelike and in flattened sprays; it is aromatic and somewhat resinous. Many arborvitaes tend to discolor in the winter. They can live to great age and develop massive buttressed trunks. The pollen- and seed-bearing cones occur on different branches of the same tree. The few-scaled cones are leathery and erect and mature the first season. The scores of cultivars offer every possible size, shape, and growth rate, in a wide range of colors, from green to yellow and bronze.

ID Features

Although the foliage of *Thuja* looks similar to that of *Chamaecyparis* (falsecypress) on first glance, the two genera can be differentiated by their dissimilar cones, the prominent white markings on most falsecypresses, and the pleasant aroma of arborvitaes.

Cultivation

Arborvitaes do best in fertile, moist, well-drained soils; some species tolerate wet conditions. They prefer full sun but do grow in part shade. They are usually shapely trees and are excellent choices for hedging because they continue to grow all season and produce new shoots after being trimmed.

Pests and Diseases

Thuja is subject to infestation with bagworms (*Thyridopteryx ephemeraeformis*), especially in warmer zones. After feeding on the foliage, the dark brown caterpillars make "bags" in which to overwinter up to a thousand eggs. The 2 in. (5 cm) long cocoonlike enclosures can look like cones to the untrained eye. A severe infestation can defoliate plants, eventually killing them. The egg-filled bags should be handpicked and destroyed from fall to spring. Insecticides can be effective if applied just after the bagworms begin to hatch. *Bacillus thuringiensis* (Bt) is effective against the larvae.

Scale can also be troublesome. They pierce plant tissue and feed on plant sap, which reduces plant vigor and causes twig dieback.

Uses

The name arborvitae ("tree of life") is a reference to the high vitamin C content in the foliage, which was used by the early explorers of the New World to prevent or treat scurvy. Arborvitaes are also an important source of food and shelter for wildlife. The wood is durable and useful.

Thuja occidentalis
Northern white-cedar, swamp-cedar
Zones 3 to 7

Generally available, popular, and very widely used for ornamental purposes, this is the species most commonly meant when people speak of arborvitaes. It is native in northern North America, from Labrador and Nova Scotia west to Manitoba and south to Massachusetts, New York, Ohio, Indiana, Illinois, and Minnesota. True to its common names, this species is found in swamps and on the banks of streams in sites where the soil is deep and humusy. It is also found at higher elevations, notably on limestone outcroppings, along the Appalachian Mountains of Virginia. It can live 200 to 300 years. In the wild, it can reach a height of 30 to 60 ft. (9 to 18 m), often with a forked trunk, but is usually below 30 ft. (9 m) in cultivation.

The northern white-cedar is a dense tree with a pyramidal shape. The branches are arranged in flat, fan-shaped sprays, more or less in one plane, and are commonly maintained to the ground. The aromatic scalelike leaves have resin glands and no white markings. The leaves are yellow-green and turn slightly bronze in the winter.

The pollen-bearing cones are small, yellow, and terminal. The seed-bearing cones are $1/4$ to $1/2$ in. (0.6 to 1.2 cm) long, upright, and oblong in clusters. They mature to a cinnamon-brown and open in the first autumn but persist through the winter. The cone scales are rounded at the tips. The fibrous bark is light red-brown (on older trees gray-brown) and shreds in long strips.

Thuja occidentalis

Thuja occidentalis seed-bearing cones

Thuja occidentalis was one of the earliest plants introduced from the New World to Europe and was grown in France before 1550. It is moderately fast-growing and very hardy; it does not do well in the southern United States. It does best in full sun in moist, well-drained soil; in shade, the plants open up and look shabby. The species is tolerant of limestone soil. It is frequently used as a hedge plant and tolerates shearing on a regular basis, though it does not sprout from old wood. The plant is usually multistemmed and therefore easily damaged by wet snow and ice storms.

The wood is soft and light but durable in contact with soil, making it useful for posts, shingles, and boxes. The First Nations peoples of eastern Canada used it to make canoes. Gardeners in suburban areas are well aware of the fondness of deer for this species. It is also grazed by snowshoe hares, porcupines, and red squirrels.

There are loads of cultivars, some nearly indistinguishable from each other. Many of them turn an unattractive brown-green in the winter; therefore, cultivars that retain their rich green color year-round are particularly valued.

'**Aurea**': globose habit, golden yellow foliage, does not require shearing, reaches 30 in. (75 cm) tall and wide.

'**Danica**': slow-growing, dense, dwarf and bushy habit, compact foliage held vertically in flat sprays, rich emerald-green, browns slightly in winter, to 18 in. (46 cm) high and wider than that.

'**Degroot's Spire**': slow-growing, rich green, very nice narrow, tightly branched, an upright form but requires attention to be sure it develops a central leader, bronzes slightly in winter.

'**Europa Gold**': slender, conical, with light yellow foliage, reaches 8 ft. (2.5 m) tall in 15 years, winter foliage is bright orange-copper.

'**Globosa**': slow-growing, dense and rounded, deep green foliage, reaches 6 ft. (1.8 m) tall.

'**Golden Globe**': slow-growing, globose, wide-spreading, soft yellow foliage, said not to scorch, reaches 4 ft. (1.2 m) tall.

Thuja occidentalis 'Aurea'

Thuja occidentalis 'Golden Globe'

'Golden Tuffet': pillow-shaped, golden orange foliage looks braided.

'Hetz Midget': extremely slow-growing, broad, rounded, dense dark green foliage turns bronze-purple in winter, reaches 3 to 4 ft. (0.9 to 1.2 m) tall.

'Holmstrup': slow-growing, medium-sized, dense and conical, vertical sprays of deep green foliage all year, eventually reaches 5 to 10 ft. (1.5 to 3 m) tall. Ideal for making a low hedge.

'Lutea': forms a narrow cone of golden yellow foliage with green interior, reaches 30 ft. (9 m) tall.

'Ohlendorfii': a round cushion of juvenile foliage with whips of adult foliage, 3 ft. (0.9 m) high.

'Rheingold': slow-growing, oval or cone-shaped, soft juvenile foliage is golden yellow in summer, deep coppery gold in winter, can be sheared, reaches up to 10 ft. (3 m) tall but usually only 2 ft. (0.6 m) tall, splits open with snow, various forms sold under this name.

'Sherwood Frost': vigorous, dense, tall, cone-shaped, light green with creamy white edges in summer, olive-green with honey-colored edges in winter, to 10 ft. (3 m) tall, splits open with snow.

'Smaragd': German for "emerald" (the color of its vertical foliage sprays), grows rapidly, reaching 15 ft. (4.5 m) tall by 4 ft. (1.2 m) wide in 15 years, stays compact, narrow, and upright, unaffected by snow or ice loads if trained to a single leader, considered by many to be the best green among the arborvitaes, maintains color year-round, good for hedging, tolerant of heat and cold, also listed as 'Emerald Green'.

'Sunkist': a dense, small, slow-growing, round-topped cone, gold yellow color in summer, burnished gold in winter, 5 to 8 ft. (1.5 to 2.5 m) tall.

'Tiny Tim': slow-growing ball, reaches 16 in. (40 cm) tall by 12 in. (30 cm) wide in eight to ten years, nice for knot gardens.

Thuja occidentalis 'Golden Tuffet'

Thuja occidentalis 'Hetz Midget'

Thuja orientalis
Oriental arborvitae, bookleaf-cypress
Zones 6 to 11

This conifer, a good one for southern climates, is sometimes listed as *Platycladus orientalis* of the monotypic genus *Platycladus*. It is distinct among the thujas for its formal habit as a large shrub or small tree, up to 25 ft. (8 m) high, and its foliage, which is held nearly vertical on erect branches; these parallel foliage sprays have earned it the common name bookleaf-cypress. The leaves are in ferny sprays and have a faint scent. The pale blue-green 3/4 in. (2 cm) cones (see photo on page 12) are larger than those of the other species, and the cone scales are thick and fleshy with stout points (recurved hooks) on their outer surface. The species is native to northern China, Manchuria, and Korea.

The oriental arborvitae is said to be very adaptable, tolerant of heat, drought, and cold. It should not be placed in a wet situation. Its numerous cultivars are becoming more widely appreciated, especially for containers and small gardens.

Thuja occidentalis 'Smaragd'

Thuja orientalis 'Aurea'

'Aurea': golden foliage, sometimes considered a group name since various forms exist.

'Collens Gold': narrow and upright with yellow-orange foliage, rapid growing, good for hedging.

'Franky Boy': dwarf and weeping with threadlike golden yellow foliage fading to yellow-green, reaches 30 in. (75 cm) tall by 24 in. (60 cm) wide in ten years.

Thuja orientalis 'Collens Gold'

Thuja orientalis 'Franky Boy'

Thuja plicata
Western red-cedar, giant arborvitae
Zones (4)5 to 7(8)

The western red-cedar (a confusing common name since the eastern red-cedar is *Juniperus virginiana*) is native from Alaska south through British Columbia and Alberta to Oregon into Idaho and Montana. Also known as canoe-cedar, it is indeed the species Lewis and Clark used for making the four large dugouts they used for transportation from Idaho to the Pacific. In those days, 800-year-old trees towering 200 ft. (60 m) tall could be found. Beautiful specimens can still be seen on Vancouver Island and other parts of British Columbia, where it is the provincial tree.

In cultivation this species can reach 50 to 70 ft. (15 to 21 m) tall. The upper branches are horizontal and the lower ones pendulous with upturned tips. The tree is majestic with a narrow crown and branches to the ground. The root system is wide-spreading. The trunk is straight and tapered and buttressed at the base. The leaves are shiny, dark yellow-green, and scalelike in drooping, ferny, flat sprays. They are pleasantly aromatic, and are usually a darker green and more polished-looking than those of *T. occidentalis*. The pollen-bearing cones are inconspicuous. The

Thuja plicata

Thuja plicata foliage and cones

Thuja plicata bark

seed-bearing cones are upright on the foliage, looking like small dried roses. The mature cone scales often have a small sharp point near the tip. The bark is thin, red-brown to gray-brown, fibrous, and shredding, forming narrow flat ridges with age.

Thuja plicata grows best in areas with a maritime climate of cool summers and mild, wet winters. It is an adaptable conifer that grows in most soil conditions without prolonged dryness.

The First Nations peoples used this species for making their celebrated totem poles (these were not religious symbols but heraldic and a record of genealogy). In fact, all parts of the Western red-cedar and another native conifer of that area, *Chamaecyparis nootkatensis*, were the main resources for their material needs: the wood, roots, bark, and branchlets were used in the construction of household necessities and textiles. Today the wood is widely used for roof shingles or any situation where durability and resistance to water decay is important.

The western red-cedar is a very handsome tree for the home landscape with its luxuriant wide-sweeping boughs. One wonders why it is not more widely used. It makes a wonderful background plant or screen. It responds well to pruning and can be trained into a lush hedge. It even tolerates some shade. And it has been observed that deer do not rush to browse on it the way they do toward *Thuja occidentalis*.

'Atrovirens': narrow and pyramidal, glossy dark green foliage all year, useful for hedging because it is said to produce new growth on old wood, tolerates wet soil and takes considerable shade, reaches 30 to 45 ft. (9 to 14 m) tall.

'Aurea': yellow-green with areas of rich old-gold tint.

'Copper Kettle': slow-growing, upright, golden-bronze foliage during cold seasons.

'Cuprea': low-spreading without a leader, rich green tipped with light yellow foliage turns

Thuja plicata 'Aurea'

copper-yellow in winter, reaches 3 ft. (0.9 m) tall. A good choice for rock gardens.

'Fastigiata': dense and compact, to 40 ft. (12 m) tall with only a 10 ft. (3 m) spread, slender ascending branches. Obviously useful for hedging.

'Green Giant': tall, narrow, and densely conical, vigorous, grows 3 to 5 ft. (0.9 to 1.5 m) a year, reaching 60 ft. (18 m) tall by 20 ft. (6 m)

Thuja plicata 'Fastigiata'

Thuja plicata 'Atrovirens'

Thuja plicata 'Cuprea'

Thuja plicata 'Whipcord'

Thuja plicata 'Zebrina' foliage

wide, glossy dark green foliage year-round is claimed, often listed as *Thuja* 'Green Giant', thought to be a hybrid between *T. standishii* and *T. plicata*.

'**Rogersii**': dense, oval, pillow-shaped, golden yellow in summer, bronze-yellow in winter, reaches 4 to 6 ft. (1.2 to 1.8 m) tall in 20 years.

'**Stoneham Gold**': a slow-growing, broad upright conical form, green in center, new growth is bright yellow in full sun, reaches 6 ft. (1.8 m) tall by 2 ft. (0.6 m) in 15 years, popular in England.

'**Whipcord**': a many-branched mounding bush with long yarnlike foliage, looks like a glossy green rag mop, bronzes in winter, reaches 5 ft. (1.5 m) tall by 4 ft. (1.2 m) wide in 20 years.

'**Zebrina**': a fast-growing tree for the open landscape, pale green foliage with creamy yellow zebra-stripe variegation all year. Stunning.

Thujopsis dolabrata foliage underside showing white "hatchet" marks

Thujopsis dolabrata
Hiba arborvitae
Zones 5 to 7

The lone species in its monotypic genus, the hiba arborvitae is native to Japan, where it is low-growing, dense, and pyramidal, ranging in size from a shrub to a 30 to 50 ft. (9 to 15 m) tall and 10 to 20 ft. (3 to 6 m) wide tree. *Thujopsis dolabrata* has many ornamental features. Its foliage is similar to that of *Thuja* but larger and broader with flat branchlets. The glossy scalelike leaves are bright green above with distinctive white markings (*dolabra* means "hatchet") underneath. The twigs branch in a staghorn-shaped pattern. The open seed-bearing cones, $1/2$ to $3/4$ in. (1.2 to 2 cm) long, resemble tiny woody flowers. The bark is reddish brown, furrowed into thin strips.

Thujopsis dolabrata tolerates cold winters and a wide range of soils but requires adequate moisture. It will grow in full sun, though it does best in partial shade with shelter and cool dampness. It has been used for hedging. This has been a plant for the collector but deserves much wider use. In Japan it provides lumber for general construction and railroad ties.

'**Aurea**': yellow-gold foliage.

Thujopsis dolabrata 'Aurea'

Thujopsis dolabrata 'Variegata'

'Nana': dwarf, a compact, mounded plant slowly reaching 3 ft. (7.5 m) tall, bright green foliage turns olive-green in winter.

'Variegata': scattered patches of creamy white, variable.

Tsuga canadensis
Eastern hemlock
Zones 3 to 7

Tsuga canadensis is one of about a dozen species in the genus *Tsuga* (hemlock), none of which are poisonous or related to the poison hemlock of classical times. That deadly brew was made from *Conium maculatum*, an herbaceous species of the family Apiaceae (carrots and parsley); *Tsuga* is a member of the unrelated family Pinaceae (pine).

The eastern hemlock is native from Nova Scotia to eastern Minnesota, and south to Maryland and Illinois. It follows the Appalachian Mountains to Georgia and northern Alabama. It thrives streamside and is frequently discovered on steep north-facing rock slopes. This large tree can reach a height of 80 ft. (24 m) or more. In the open it presents a very graceful appearance, dense and branched to the ground; in crowded stands, where it is commonly seen, it is free of lower branches.

The soft ½ in. (1.2 cm) needles are arranged spirally on the stem but often appear two-ranked. They are flat, lustrous dark green, and have two white lines on the lower surface. They remain on the tree for up to ten years. A row of smaller leaves along the upper surface of the twigs appears to be flipped over—flat on the stem, with the silver bands showing. This is a useful ID feature.

Tsuga canadensis

The ½ to ¾ in. (1.2 to 2 cm) long cones hang down on short stalks. They are among the smallest of all cones and mature in one season but remain on the tree until the following year. Trees don't start producing seeds until they are several decades old; they take 15 to 20 years to reach 30 to 40 ft. (9 to 12 m) in height. The bark is red-brown to gray-brown at maturity with long fissures and scaly ridges.

This slow-growing conifer prefers cool, moist, woodland conditions. It is damaged by salt and does not tolerate air pollution. Seedlings are able to establish under the canopy of mature trees.

Tsuga canadensis foliage and seed-bearing cones

Tsuga canadensis makes a very desirable ornamental plant for the landscape. It is shade-tolerant and fine-textured, has good foliage color, and can be shaped into an elegant hedge. This species lends a graceful touch among stiffer-looking conifers. It is somewhat shallow-rooted and can be felled by strong winds. There are dozens of named cultivars in the trade, but the species itself is not widely planted in Europe.

Vast native stands of this species were harvested for the tannin-rich bark, which is used for tanning leather. The brittle wood is not durable and is used primarily for making boxes and as pulpwood. The foliage provides food, nesting, and cover for wildlife, and numerous birds, especially warblers, seek out the seeds. The eastern hemlock is the state tree of Pennsylvania.

This beautiful conifer is threatened by *Adelges tsugae*, the hemlock woolly adelgid, which has since the mid 20th century spread relentlessly throughout the eastern United States. Recent climate changes with warmer winters have accelerated the problem. This sap-sucking insect infests eastern hemlocks of all ages, causing reduction in new shoot development, thinning of foliage, branch dieback, and the eventual death of the tree. An infestation is easy to recognize: the egg sacs of these insects look like bits of cotton clinging to the undersides of the needles. Horticultural oil and insecticidal soap give some control of this pest, but there is no known effective way to prevent its spread. The fear is that *Tsuga canadensis* mortality could reach 100 percent, affecting forest composition and the ecology of wildlife habitats. Potential substitutes for this hemlock include *Chamaecyparis nootkatensis*, *C. obtusa*, *Cryptomeria japonica*, *Picea orientalis*, *Thuja plicata*, and *T. plicata* 'Green Giant'.

'Bennett': slow-growing dwarf, spreading mound with pendulous branch tips, dark green foliage, becomes 2 ft. (0.6 m) tall by 4 ft. (1.2 m) wide in ten years.

'Cole's Prostrate': slow-growing, mat-forming with branches extending flat along the ground, silver-gray center branches become exposed with maturity, grows 3 ft. (0.9 m) in 20 years. Useful for shady rock gardens or for vest-pocket gardens.

'Everitt's Golden': slow-growing stiff small tree with ascending branches, tight needles, golden yellow early in season, green to bronze by fall, needs afternoon shade, also called 'Everitt Golden'.

'Gentsch White': slow-growing shrub, white-tipped or variegated foliage, benefits from occasional shearing, reaches 2 ft. (0.6 m) tall by 3 ft. (0.9 m) wide.

'Jeddeloh': low-spreading nestlike bush with pendulous branch tips, mediuma green, reaches 4 to 5 ft. (1.2 to 1.5 m) tall, similar to 'Bennett', popular in Europe.

Tsuga canadensis 'Bennett'

Tsuga canadensis 'Gentsch White'

Tsuga canadensis 'Summer Snow'

'**Kelsey's Weeping**': fast-growing, irregular weeper, 2 ft. (0.6 m) tall by 5 ft. (1.5 m) wide in ten years.

'**Pendula**' **(Sargent's hemlock):** overlapping, pendulous branches, a magnificent spreading lawn specimen after several decades.

'**Summer Snow**': fast-growing, upright and conical, green foliage with white tips.

Wollemia nobilis
Wollemi-pine
Zone 10

This recently described conifer (not a pine, of course) was found in 1994 by an observant Australian Park Service officer and explorer, David Noble, growing in a wet and sheltered gorge in the Wollemi National Park, a mountainous area northwest of Sydney in New South Wales. The specific epithet *nobilis* honors both the tree's majestic qualities and its discoverer. It is reported that the wild population consists of about three dozen plants and hundreds of seedlings.

The tree is pyramidal and grows about 12 in. (30 cm) a year. It will reach more than 100 ft. (30 m) at maturity. The dark green leaves are distinctive; they are arranged in four ranks. The tree tends to shed whole branches rather than individual leaves. New growth appears from the base of trees that have been cut or damaged by nature. The pollen- and seed-bearing cones appear on the same tree. The seed-bearing cones are at the very top of the trees. The bark has been described as resembling bubbling chocolate.

There seems to be no genetic variation within the Wollemi-pine populations; this monotypic genus is related to the ancient genus *Araucaria* (monkey puzzle tree, Norfolk Island pine) and is believed to have grown in vast forests in Australia at one time. Efforts are underway to propagate the plant and initiate worldwide distribution, with royalties from sales going to support conservation of this and other rare and endangered plant species. The Wollemi-pine will be a conservatory plant for much of North America and northern Europe.

Wollemia nobilis habit

Wollemia nobilis foliage

NURSERY SOURCES

United States

Arrowhead Alpines
1310 North Gregory Road
Fowlerville, Michigan 48836
517 223 3581
www.arrowheadalpines.com

Bethlehem Nursery
66 Jackson Lane
Bethlehem, Connecticut 06751
www.bethlehemnursery.com

Bloom River Gardens
39744 Deerhorn Road
Springfield, Oregon 97478
541 726 8997
www.bloomriver.com

Coenosium Gardens
4412 354th Street East
Eatonville, Washington 98328
360 832 8655
www.coenosium.com

Collector's Nursery
16804 NE 102nd Avenue
Battle Ground, Washington 98604
360 574 3832
www.collectorsnursery.com

Forest Farm Nursery
990 Tetherow
Williams, Oregon 97544
541 846 7269
www.forestfarm.com

Gee Farms
14928 Bunkerhill Road
Stockbridge, Michigan 49285
517 769 6772
www.geefarms.com

Girard Nurseries
6839 North Ridge East
Geneva, Ohio 44041
440 466 2881
www.girardnurseries.com

Greer Gardens
1280 Goodpasture Island Road
Eugene, Oregon 97401
800 548 0111
www.greergardens.com

Porterhowse Farms
41370 SE Thomas Road
Sandy, Oregon 97055
503 668 5834
www.porterhowse.com

RareFind Nursery
957 Patterson Road
Jackson, New Jersey 08527
732 833 0613
www.rarefindnursery.com

Rich's Foxwillow Pines Nursery
11618 McConnell Road
Woodstock, Illinois 60098
815 338 7442
www.richsfoxwillowpines.com

Siskiyou Rare Plant Nursery
2115 Talent Avenue
Talent, Oregon 97540
541 535 7103
www.siskiyourareplantnursery.com

Suncrest Gardens
816 Holly Pike
Mt. Holly Springs, Pennsylvania 17065
717 486 5142
www.suncrest-gardens.com

Twombly Nursery
163 Barn Hill Road
Monroe, Connecticut 06468
203 261 2133
www.twomblynursery.com

Wolf-Run Nursery
29 Klapperthal Road
Reading, Pennsylvania 19606
610 779 5717
www.wolfrunnursery.com

International

Bruns Pflanzen Export
Johann-Bruns-Allee 1
26160 Bad Zwischenahn
Germany
04403 60 10
www.bruns.de

Cedar Lodge Nursery
63 Egmont Road, RD 2
New Plymouth
New Zealand
06 755 0369
www.conifers.co.nz

Hachmann Baumschule
Brunnenstrasse 68
25355 Barmstedt
Germany
04123 20 55
www.hachmann.de

zu Jeddeloh Pflanzenhandels
Wischenstrasse 7
26188 Edewecht
Germany
04405 91 80 0
www.jeddeloh.de

Kenwith Nursery
Beaford Winkleigh
Devon EX19 8NT
England
01805 603274
www.kenwithnursery.co.uk

Lime Cross Nursery
Herstmonceus
Hailsham
East Sussex BN27 4RS
England
01323 833229
www.limecross.co.uk

Uwe Horstmann Baumschulen
Rotenburger Strasse 60
29640 Schneverdingen
Germany
05193 44 68
www.tsuga-shop.de

GLOSSARY

appressed pressed closely against an object
aril a fleshy pulp that surrounds the seed and is open at the apex
bonsai the art of growing and shaping miniature trees in a shallow tray
candle soft new growth characteristic of pines
catkin a compact cluster of flowers, often drooping and often single-sexed
columnar tall and narrow
conifer cone-bearing; a woody plant that bears seeds in a cone rather than a flower
deciduous having foliage that does not remain on the plant year-round but instead drops to the ground in winter
dioecious producing pollen-bearing cones and seed-bearing cones on separate trees
dragon's-eye pine any of a group of pines with predominantly green needles marked by bands of usually yellow color and thus resembling the eye of a dragon when viewed closely
espalier a plant trained to grow flat against a wall
evergreen having foliage that remains green year-round
exfoliating said of bark peeling off in shreds or thin layers
fastigiate having ascending branches
glaucous covered with a fine whitish substance
globose rounded
intergeneric hybrid a cross involving parents from two different genera
lateral attached to the side, not at the apex

leader the main (and usually highest) growing stem of a plant
knees woody projections produced by cypresses growing in wet habitats and formed of tree roots that come above the surface of the soil to help anchor the tree
monoecious producing both pollen- and seed-bearing cones on the same tree
monotypic genus a genus comprising a single species
pendulous with weeping branches
pistillate cones female, seed-bearing cones
poodled to be pruned in a decorative pattern resembling that of a well-groomed poodle
prostrate growing close to and spreading over the ground
pubescent covered with soft, short hairs
pyramidal conical, broad at base, narrowing and tapering to the top
staminate cones male, pollen-bearing cones
standard a plant with an upright stem or one trained that way
stomata minute pores in the epidermis of a needle, usually on the underside
terminal attached at the tip or growing point
topiary the art of shaping plants into ornamental figures
understock the root plant onto which a stock has been grafted to produce a new plant
witches' brooms congested bundles of usually small-needled growths that are attached to normal branches, particularly those of pines and spruces

FURTHER READING

Arno, Stephen F. 1977. *Northwest Trees*. The Mountaineers: Seattle, Washington.

Bitner, Richard L. 2007. *Conifers for Gardens: An Illustrated Encyclopedia*. Timber Press: Portland, Oregon.

Bloom, Adrian. 2002. *Gardening with Conifers*. Firefly Books: Buffalo, New York.

Blouin, Glen. 2001. *An Eclectic Guide to Trees East of the Rockies*. Boston Mills Press: Erin, Ontario.

Brooklyn Botanic Garden. 2001. *Growing Conifers: Four-Season Plants*. Brooklyn Botanic Garden: New York.

Cope, Edward A. 1993. *Native and Cultivated Conifers of Northeastern North America: A Guide*. Cornell University: Ithaca, New York.

Cutler, Sandra McLean. 1997. *Dwarf and Unusual Conifers Coming of Age: A Guide to Mature Garden Conifers*. Barton-Bradley Crossroads: North Olmsted, Ohio.

Dirr, Michael A. 2009. *Manual of Woody Landscape Plants*. Stipes: Champaign, Illinois.

Eckenwalder, James E. 2009. *Conifers of the World: The Complete Reference*. Timber Press: Portland, Oregon.

Farjon, Aljos. 2008. *A Natural History of Conifers*. Timber Press: Portland, Oregon.

Grimm, William Carey. 2001. *The Illustrated Book of Trees: The Comprehensive Field Guide to More Than 250 Trees of Eastern North American*. Rev. ed. Stackpole Books: Mechanicsburg, Pennsylvania.

Hillier Nurseries. 2007. *The Hillier Manual of Trees and Shrubs*. 3rd ed. David & Charles: Devon, England.

Lanner, Ronald M. 2002. *Conifers of California*. Cachuma Press: Los Olivos, California.

Powell, Graham R. 2009. *Lives of Conifers: A Comparative Account of the Coniferous Trees*. John Hopkins University Press: Baltimore, Maryland.

INDEX

Bold-faced numbers indicate photo pages.

Abies, 27–35
Abies concolor, 28–31, **29**
  'Blue Cloak', 30
  'Candicans', **30**
  'Compacta', 30
  'Conica', **30**
  'Glauca Compacta', 30
  'Wattezii', 30, **31**
  'Wattezii Prostrata', 30
  'Winter Gold', 31
Abies koreana, **31**, 31–32
  'Cis', 32
  'Goldener Traum', 32
  'Prostrate Beauty', **32**
  'Silberkugel', 32
  'Silberlocke', **32**
  'Starker's Dwarf', 32
Abies lasiocarpa, 32–33
  var. *arizonica*, 33
  var. *arizonica* 'Compacta', **33**
  'Arizona Compacta', 33
  'Martha's Vineyard', 33
  'Mulligan's Dwarf', 33
Abies nordmanniana, **12**, **33**, 33–34
  'Barabits', 34
  'Barabits' Compact', 34
  'Barabits' Spreader', 34
  'Golden Spreader', **34**
Abies pinsapo, 34–35, **35**
  'Aurea', 35
  'Glauca', **35**
  'Horstmann', 35
Alaska-cedar, 58–61
Araucaria araucana, 35–37, **36**
arborvitae, 193–207
arborvitae, giant, 201–207
arborvitae, Hiba, 207–208
arborvitae, oriental, 198–200

bald-cypress, 182–187
bookleaf-cypress, 198–200

Calocedrus decurrens, **6**, **37**, 37–39
  'Aureovariegata', 39
  'Berrima Gold', **38**, 39

'Maupin Glow', **38**, 39
cedar, 39–51
cedar, Atlas, 40–43
cedar, deodar, 43–49
cedar, Himalayan, 43–49
cedar, weeping blue Atlas, 43
cedar of Lebanon, 49–51
Cedrus, 39–51
Cedrus atlantica, 40–43
  'Aurea', 41
  'Aurea Robusta', **41**
  'Cheltenham', **42**
  'Fastigiata', **42**
  'Glauca Pendula', **43**
Cedrus deodara, 43–49
  'Aurea', 44, **49**
  'Devinely Blue', 44
  'Feelin' Blue', **44**
  'Glacier', **44**
  'Gold Cone', 44, **45**
  'Gold Horizon', 44, 46
  'Golden Horizon', 44, **46**
  'Karl Fuchs', **10**, **46**, **49**
  'Kashmir', 46
  'Pygmaea', 46
  'Pygmy', 46
  'Raywood's Prostrate Dwarf', **46**
  'Roman Gold', 46, **47**
  'Shalimar', **46**, 49
  'Snow Sprite', **48**, 49
  'Wells Golden', 46
Cedrus libani, 39–51
  'Blue Angel', **50**, 51
  'Brevifolia', 51
  'Glauca Pendula', 51
  'Green Prince', 51
  subsp. *stenocoma*, **51**
Cephalotaxus, 52–54
Cephalotaxus harringtonia, 52–54
  var. *drupacea* 'Duke Gardens', **52**
  'Fastigiata', **53**
  'Korean Gold', **53**
  'Prostrata', **54**
Chamaecyparis, 54–70
Chamaecyparis lawsoniana, **55**, 55–58, **56**
  'Alumnii', 57

INDEX

'Green Globe', **56**, 57
'Oregon Blue', **57**
'Pelt's Blue, 57
'Pembury Blue', **57**
'Schneeball', **58**
'Silver Threads', 58
'Stardust', 58
'Yvonne', 58
Chamaecyparis nootkatensis, 58–61
  'Aurea', 59
  'Green Arrow', **59**
  'Jubilee', 59
  'Pendula', **60, 61**
  'Strict Weeper', **61**
  'Strict Weeping', **61**
  'Van den Akker', 61
  'Variegata', **61**
Chamaecyparis obtusa, **16**, 62–65
  'Compacta', 63
  'Coralliformis', **63**
  'Crippsii', **63**
  'Elmwood Gold', **63**
  'Fernspray Gold', 64
  'Filicoides', 64
  'Gracilis', 64
  'Green Cushion', **64**
  'Intermedia', 64
  'Jean Iseli', **64**
  'Kamakurahiba', 64
  'Kosteri', 64
  'Little Marky', **64**
  'Meroke Twin', 65
  'Minima', **65**
  'Nana Aurea', 65
  'Nana Gracilis', **65**
  'Opaal', **65**
  'Pygmaea', 65
  'Reis Dwarf', 65
  'Tempelhof', 65
Chamaecyparis pisifera, 66–70
  'Boulevard', **67**, 68
  'Curly Tops', 68
  'Filifera', 68
  'Filifera Aurea', **68**
  'Filifera Aureovariegata', 69
  'Gold Spangle', **69**
  'Golden Mop', **70**
  'Lemon Thread', **70**
  'Snow', 70
  'Sungold', **70**

  'White Pygmy', **70**
chile-pine, 35–37
China-fir, 76–77
Cryptomeria japonica, 71–75
  'Bandai-sugi', 71
  'Barabits' Gold', 71
  'Benjamin Franklin', 71
  'Black Dragon', 71
  'Cristata', **72**, 73
  'Elegans Nana', **72**, 73
  'Globosa Nana', **72**, 73
  'Gyokuryu', 73
  'Knaptonensis', 73
  'Koshyi', 73
  'Rein's Dense Jade', **73**
  'Sekkan-sugi', **73**
  'Spiralis', **74**
  'Spiraliter Falcata', **74**, 75
  'Tansu', **74**, 75
  'Vilmorin Gold', 75
  'Vilmoriniana', 75
  'Yoshino', **75**
Cunninghamia lanceolata, 76–77
  'Chanson's Gift', 76
  'Glauca', **76**
  'Little Leo', 77
×*Cupressocyparis leylandii*, 77–79
  'Gold Rider', **77**
  'Green Spire', 78
  'Harlequin', **78**
  'Naylor's Blue', **78**, 79
  'Silver Dust', **78**, 79
  'Star Wars', 79
Cupressus, 79–83
Cupressus arizonica, 79–81
  'Arctic', 81
  'Blue Ice', **80**, 81
  'Blue Pyramid', **81**
  var. *glabra*, 79
  'Golden Pyramid', **81**
  'Sapphire Skies', **81**
Cupressus glabra, 79
Cupressus macrocarpa, 82
  'Aurea', 82
  'Lutea', **82**
Cupressus sempervirens, 82–83
  var. *stricta*, 82
  'Swane's Gold', 83
  'Totem', **83**
  'Totem Pole', 83

INDEX

cypress, 79–83
cypress, Arizona, 79–81
cypress, Italian, 82–83
cypress, Leyland, 77–79
cypress, Monterey, 82
cypress, Siberian, 116
cypress, smooth, 79

Douglas-fir, 176–177

falsecypress, 54–70
falsecypress, Hinoki, 62–65
falsecypress, Lawson, 55–58
falsecypress, Nootka, 58–61
fir, 27–35
fir, alpine, 32–33
fir, concolor, 28–31
fir, corkbark, 33
fir, Korean, 31–32
fir, Nordmann, 33–34
fir, Rocky Mountain, 33
fir, Spanish, 34–35

Ginkgo, 83–86
Ginkgo biloba, 83–86, **84**
   'Autumn Gold', 85
   'Chi-chi', 85
   'Mariken', **85**
   'Princeton Sentry', 85
   'Saratoga', **86**
   'Tremonia', 86
   'Tubifolia', **86**
   'Tubiformis', 86
golden-larch, **8**, 175–176, **176**

hemlock, 208–213
hemlock, eastern, 208–213

incense-cedar, 37–39

Japanese-cedar, 71–75
juniper, 86–106
juniper, Andorra, 98
juniper, Chinese, 88–92
juniper, common, 92–95
juniper, creeping, 96–99
juniper, flaky, 102–103
juniper, garden, 100
juniper, hedgehog, 93

juniper, Hollywood, 90
juniper, Irish, 94
juniper, Pfitzer, 99–100
juniper, Rocky Mountain, 100–102
juniper, savin, 86
juniper, shore, 95–96
juniper, singleseed, 102–103
juniper, Waukegan, 97
Juniperus, 86–106
Juniperus chinensis, 88–92
   'Aurea', **88**
   'Blaauw', 88
   'Blue Alps', 88
   'Daub's Frosted', 88, **89**
   'Gold Sovereign', 88, **89**
   'Gold Star', **90**
   'Kaizuka', 90
   'Obelisk', 90
   'Old Gold', **90**
   'Plumosa Aurea', 90, **91**
   'Robust Green', 90
   'San Jose', 90
   'Saybrook Gold', **92**
   'Stricta', 92
   'Torulosa', 90
   'Variegated Kaizuka', **92**
Juniperus communis, 92–95
   'Berkshire', 93
   'Compressa', **93**
   'Echiniformis', 93
   'Gold Cone', **93**
   'Green Carpet', 93, **94**
   'Haverbeck', 90, **94**
   'Hemispherica', 93
   'Hibernica', 94
   'Hornibrookii', 94, **95**
   'Horstmann', 94
   'Pencil Point', 94, **95**
   'Prostrata', 94
   'Repanda', 95
   'Sentinel', 95
Juniperus conferta, 95–96
   'Blue Lagoon', **96**
   'Blue Pacific', **96**
   'Silver Mist', 96
Juniperus horizontalis, 96–99
   'Bar Harbor', 97
   'Blue Chip', 97
   'Blue Rug', 99
   'Douglasii', **97**

INDEX

'Golden Carpet', 97
'Green Acres', 97
'Icee Blue', **97**
'Limeglow', **98**
'Monber', **97**
'Mother Lode', **98**
'Plumosa', 98
'Prince of Wales', 99
'Wiltonii', 98, **99**
'Youngstown', 99
Juniperus ×*media*, 86
Juniperus ×*pfitzeriana*, 99–100
   'Gold Coast', **99**
Juniperus procumbens, 100
   'Nana', **100**
Juniperus scopulorum, 100–102
   'Blue Arrow', **101**, 102
   'Skyrocket', 102
Juniperus sabina, 86
Juniperus squamata, 102–103
   'Blue Carpet', **102**, 103
   'Blue Star', 103
   'Holger', 103
   'Meyeri', 103
Juniperus virginiana, 103–106
   'Blue Arrow', 105
   'Burkii', **105**
   'Canaertii', **106**
   'Corcorcor', 106
   'Emerald Sentinel', 106
   'Grey Owl', **106**
   'Hillspire', 106
   'Kosteri', 106

larch, 107–113
larch, American, 112–113
larch, European, 107–110
larch, Japanese, 110–111
Larix, 107–113
Larix decidua, 107–110, **108**
   'Horstmann Recurved', **109**
   'Pendula', 109
   'Puli', **109**
   'Varied Directions', 109
Larix ×*eurolepsis*, 109, **110**
Larix kaempferi, 110–111, **111**
   'Blue Rabbit', 111
   'Blue Rabbit Weeping', 111
   'Diane', 111
   'Diana', 111

'Pendula', **111**
'Stiff Weeping', 111
'Wolterdingen', 111
Larix laricina, 112–113
   'Blue Sparkler', **112**, 113
   'Craftsbury Flats', **113**
Lawson-falsecypress, 55–58
Libocedrus decurrens, 37–39

maidenhair tree, 83–86
Metasequoia glyptostroboides, **15**, **22**, **114**,
   114–115, **115**
   'Gold Rush', 116
   'Ogon', **2**, **115**
   'Sheridan Spire', 115
Microbiota decussata, **116**
monkey puzzle tree, 35–37

Nootka-cypress, 58–61

Picea, 116–147
Picea abies, 118–130, **120**
   'Acrocona', **121**
   'Cincinnata', 121
   'Clanbrassiliana', 121
   'Cranstonii', 121
   'Echiniformis', **121**
   'Elegantissima', **122**, 123
   'Formanek', 123
   'Frohburg', 123
   'Gold Drift', **123**
   'Gregoryana', 123
   'Inversa', **124**
   'Little Gem', **124**, **133**
   'Maxwellii', 124
   'Mucronata', 124
   'Nidiformis', 124, **125**
   f. *pendula*, 127
   'Pendula', 124, **125**, **126**
   'Perry's Gold', **127**
   'Procumbens', **128**
   'Prostrata', 128
   'Pumila', **128**
   'Pygmaea', 128
   'Reflexa', 128
   'Repens', 128, **129**
   'Saint James', 129
   f. *virgata*, **129**
   'Virgata', **129**
   'Wingle's Weeper', **130**

Picea glauca, 130–135
  'Alberta Globe', 130
  'Albertiana Conica', 133
  'Blue Planet', 130, **131**
  'Cecilia', 132
  'Conica', **132**
  'Daisy's White', 133
  'Echiniformis', **132**, 133
  'Gnome', 133
  'Jean's Dilly', **133**
  'Laurin', 133
  'Little Globe', 133
  'Pixie', **133**
  'Pixie Dust', **134**, 135
  'Rainbow's End', **135**
  'Sander's Blue', **135**
  'Zuckerhut', 135
Picea omorika, 135–139
  'Aurea', 136
  'Nana', **136**
  'Pendula', 136, **137**
  'Pendula Bruns', **138**, 139
  'Pimoko', 139
  'Treblitzsch', 139
Picea orientalis, 139–141
  'Atrovirens', 141
  'Aureospicata', **140**, 141
  'Barnes', 141
  'Bergman's Gem', 141
  'Connecticut Turnpike', **140**, 141
  'Gowdy', 141
  'Nana', 141
  'Nutans', 141
  'Skylands', **141**
  'Tom Thumb', **141**
Picea pungens, 141–147
  'Baby Blueyes', **142**
  'Blue Pearl', 142
  'Compacta', **142**
  'Fat Albert', 142
  'Glauca Compacta', 142
  'Glauca Pendula', 145
  'Globosa', 142
  'Hoopsii', 142, **143**
  'Koster', 145
  'Kosteri', 145
  'Montgomery', **145**
  'Pendula', **144**, 145
  'Saint Mary', 145
  'Saint Mary's Broom', 145
  'Spring Blast', **145**
  'Spring Ghost', **146**, 147
  'Thomsen', 147
  'Thuem', 147
  'Thume', 147
  'Walnut Glen', 147
pine, **21**, 147–175
pine, Austrian, 163–164
pine, Bosnian, 158–161
pine, bristlecone, 151
pine, eastern white, 167–171
pine, Himalayan, 174–174
pine, jack, 151–152
pine, Japanese black, 173–174
pine, Japanese red, 155–157
pine, Japanese white, 164–167
pine, lacebark, 152
pine, limber, 157–158
pine, mugo, 161–163
pine, Rocky Mountain bristlecone, 151
pine, Scotch, 171–172
pine, Scots, 171–172
pine, Swiss stone, 152–155
pine, Weymouth, 167–171
Pinus, 147–175
Pinus aristata, 151
  'Sherwood Compact', **150**, 151
Pinus banksiana, 151–152
  'Chippewa', 151
  'Uncle Fogy', **152**
  'Wisconsin', 152
Pinus bungeana, **152**
  'Silver Ghost', 152
Pinus cembra, 152–155
  'Blue Mound', **154**, 155
  'Chalet', 155
  'Nana', 155
  'Stricta', 155
Pinus densiflora, 155–157
  'Alice Verkade', 155
  'Golden Ghost', **155**
  'Jane Kluis', **156**
  'Low Glow', 156
  'Oculus-draconis', **156**
  'Pendula', 156, **157**
  'Tanyosho', 156
  'Umbraculifera', 156
Pinus flexilis, 157–158
  'Vanderwolf's Pyramid', **158**
Pinus griffithii, 174–175

INDEX

Pinus leucodermis, 158–161
  'Compact Gem', 159
  'Emerald Arrow', 159
  'Iseli Fastigiate', **159**
  'Mint Truffle', 160, 161
  'Schmidtii', 161
  'Smidtii', 161
Pinus mugo, **161**, 161–163
  'Big Tuna', 163
  'Corley's Mat', 163
  'Gnom', 163
  'Jakobsen', 163
  'Mitsch Mini', **162**, 163
  'Mops', **162**, 163
  'Ophir', 163
  'Sherwood Compact', 163
  'Slowmound', **162**, 163
  'Winter Gold', 163
Pinus nigra, 163–164
  'Arnold Sentinel', 164
  'Globosa', 164
  'Helga', **164**
  'Hornibrookiana', 164
Pinus parviflora, 164–167
  'Adcock's Dwarf', **165**
  'Aoba-jo', 165
  'Bergman', 165
  'Brevifolia', 165
  'Glauca Nana', 167
  'Goldilocks', **166**, 167
  'Ogon Janome', **167**
  'Tani-mano-uki', 167
Pinus strobus, 167–171
  'Blue Shag', 168
  'Coney Island', 168
  'Contorta', **168**
  'Fastigiata', **169**
  'Horsford', 169
  'Louie', **170**, 171
  'Merrimack', 171
  'Minuta', **171**
  'Pendula', 171
  'Radiata', 171
  'Sea Urchin', 171
  'Torulosa', 171
  'UConn', 171
Pinus sylvestris, 171–172
  'Albyns', 172
  'Aurea', 172
  'Beuvronensis', 172

  'Globosa Viridis', 172
  'Hillside Creeper', 172
  'Watereri', 172, **173**
Pinus thunbergii, 173–174
  'Banshosho', 174
  'Oculus-draconis', **174**
  'Thunderhead', **174**
Platycladus orientalis,
plum-yew, 52–54
plum-yew, Japanese, 52–54
Pinus wallichiana, 174–175
  'Nana', 175
  'Zebrina', **175**
pond-cypress, 183–184
Port-Orford-cedar, 55–58
Pseudolarix amabilis, **8**, 175–176, **176**
Pseudotsuga menziesii, 176–177
  'Fastigiata', 177
  'Graceful Grace', 177
  'Pendula', **177**
  'Pumila', **177**

red-cedar, eastern, 103–106
red-cedar, western, 201–207
redwood, dawn, 114–115
Rocky Mountain fir, compact, 33

Sargent's hemlock, 213
sawara-cypress, 66–70
Sciadopitys verticillata, 178–179
  'Golden Rush', 179
  'Grüne Kugel', 179
  'Joe Kozey', **178**, 179
  'Ossorio Gold', **179**
  'Sternschnuppe', 179
  'Wintergreen', **179**
sequoia, giant, 180–182
Sequoiadendron giganteum, **180**–182
  'Blauer Eichzwerg', 181
  'Glaucum', 181
  'Hazel Smith', **181**
  'Pendulum', **182**
spruce, 116–147
spruce, bird's nest, 124
spruce, Colorado, 141–147
spruce, dwarf Alberta, 132
spruce, Norway, 118–130
spruce, oriental, 139–141
spruce, Serbian, 135–139
spruce, snake branch, 129

INDEX

spruce, white, 130–135
swamp-cedar, 194–198

tamarack, 113
Taxodium, 182–183
Taxodium ascendens, **183**, 183–184, **184**
  var. *nutans*, 183–184
  'Nutans', 184
  'Prairie Sentinel', 184
Taxodium distichum, 184–187, **185**
  'Cascade Falls', **186**, 187
  'Peve Minaret', **187**
  'Peve Yellow', **187**
  'Secrest', **186**, 187
Taxus, 188–193
Taxus baccata, **188**, **190**–192
  'Amersfoort', 191
  'David', **190**, 191
  'Dovastonii Aurea', 191
  'Fastigiata Robusta', 191
  'Repandens', **191**
  'Semperaurea', 191
  'Standishii', **192**
Taxus cuspidata, 192–193
  'Aurescens', **192**, 193
Taxus ×*media*, 193
  'Beanpole', **193**
  'Flushing', 193
  'Helleri', 193
  'Hicksii', 193
Thuja, 193–207
Thuja 'Green Giant', 205
Thuja occidentalis, 194–198, **195**
  'Aurea', 196, **197**
  'Danica', 196
  'Degroot's Spire', 196
  'Emerald Green', 198
  'Europa Gold', 196
  'Globosa', 196
  'Golden Globe', 196, **197**
  'Golden Tuffet', 198, **198**
  'Hetz Midget', **198**
  'Holmstrup', 198
  'Lutea', 198
  'Ohlendorfii', 198
  'Rheingold', 198
  'Sherwood Frost', 198
  'Smaragd', 198, **199**
  'Sunkist', 198
  'Tiny Tim', 198

Thuja orientalis, **12**, 198–200
  'Aurea', **200**
  'Collens Gold', 200, **201**
  'Franky Boy', 200, **201**
Thuja plicata, 201–207, **202**
  'Atrovirens', 204, **205**
  'Aurea', **204**
  'Copper Kettle', 204
  'Cuprea', 204, **205**
  'Fastigiata', **205**
  'Green Giant', 205
  'Rogersii', 207
  'Stoneham Gold', 207
  'Whipcord', **206**, 207
  'Zebrina', **206**, 207
Thujopsis dolabrata, 207–208
  'Aurea', **207**
  'Nana', 208
  'Variegata', **208**
Tsuga, 208–213
Tsuga canadensis, 208–213, **209**
  'Bennett', 210, **211**
  'Cole's Prostrate', 210
  'Everitt's Golden', 211
  'Gentsch White', **211**
  'Jeddeloh', 211
  'Kelsey Weeping', 213
  'Pendula', 213
  'Summer Snow', **212**, 213

umbrella-pine, 178–179

white-cedar, northern, 194198
Wollemia nobilis, **213**
Wollemi-pine, 213

Xanthocyparis nootkatensis, 5861

yellow-cedar, 58
yellow-cypress, 58
yew, 188193
yew, English, 190192
yew, hybrid, 193
yew, Japanese, 192193